SHUGBOROUGH

John Martin Robinson

THE NATIONAL TRUST

I am grateful to the following for help with the
compilation of this guidebook:
The Earl of Lichfield, Anthony du Boulay, Julian Gibbs,
F. St John Gore, Julie Grymel, Gervase Jackson-Stops,
Margaret Lancaster, Alastair Laing, Christopher Nicholson,
Alison Rendle, Pamela Sambrook, Margaret Willes.

John Martin Robinson

Photographs: by gracious permission of Her Majesty the Queen page
51; *Country Life* pages 40, 41 above and below, 42; Elder Brethren of
Trinity House/Courtauld Institute of Art page 35; Cliff Guttridge
page 68; Lord Lichfield pages 36, 62, 77, 82, 90; The National
Maritime Museum, London pages 8, 14 above and below; The
National Portrait Gallery, London page 25; NT/John Bethell page
57; NT/A. C. Cooper page 50; NT/Mark Fiennes page 73; NT/
Angelo Hornak back cover; NT/Christopher Hurst front cover,
pages 29, 49; NT/Eric Pelham page 38; NT/J. E. Rackham page 46;
NT/Geoffrey Shakerley pages 6, 15, 16, 20, 28, 29 above, 59, 63, 66;
NT/Jeremy Whitaker pages 21, 58, 60, 65, 70; NT/Mike Williams
pages 4, 12, 18, 19, 23, 27 below, 30, 31, 37, 39, 44, 47, 48, 53, 54, 55,
76, 78, 80, 81, 84, 86, 87, 89; Trustees of the Royal Botanic Gardens,
Kew page 10; Staffordshire County Council page 39; Board of
Trustees of the Victoria and Albert Museum page 33.

Designed by James Shurmer

Phototypeset in Monotype Bembo Series 270
by SPAN Graphics Ltd, Crawley, West Sussex (6665)

Colour reproduction by Aculith 76, Barnet, Hertfordshire

Print managed by Centurion Press (JBP)
for the National Trust, 36 Queen Anne's Gate, London SW1H 9AS

CONTENTS

Introduction   *page* 5

Chapter One Admiral Lord Anson   7

Chapter Two Thomas Anson and the Creation of a Seat   18

Chapter Three Shugborough under Viscount Anson   34

Chapter Four The Great Sale and Revival   45

Chapter Five The Twentieth Century   53

Chapter Six The House   55

Chapter Seven Garden and Park   79

Plan of the Garden and Park   91

Bibliography   92

Family Tree   93

Index   94

Plan of the House   *inside back cover*

The east front of Shugborough today

INTRODUCTION
by Lord Lichfield

As a small boy Shugborough appeared to me to be a labyrinth of mystery and adventure. All the different departments held their own individual spells for my sister and me, and though close to one another, we invariably went our separate ways during the days when we left the nursery.

There was the grand part of the house which seemed, when we were very small, to be altogether too imposing. Then there was the nursery where we spent our nights and rainy days. So for the most part we escaped to where the staff would be busying themselves with their various skills, and it was there that we learnt what really went into the running of a great house. Seeing this, our elders took an opportunity of allowing us to understudy them, not I hope to provide unpaid labour, but so that we might learn at least a little of their separate roles and skills. Thus, after the age of eight, when we returned from our boarding schools, we would be detailed to watch and supposedly help a key department, with my sister concentrating on the domestic side and myself on the outdoor staff. She has since become the most successful party organiser in the country and was doubtless helped by what she learnt in the kitchens, laundry, butler's pantry, scullery, and with the ladies' maid and head housekeeper.

I was fortunate enough to follow, with wide-eyed fascination and growing respect, the cabinetmaker, plumber, house painter, keeper, electrician, head chauffeur and, most important of all, the head forester and head keeper. From the two last, I learnt a deep-rooted love of the countryside and, most particularly, of the Shugborough Estate and Cannock Chase.

Sometimes today I wish that my three children could experience the tranquillity that pervaded the park when I was young, where after a fortnight of snow ours were the only footprints in our favourite hidden parts of the garden. But change there had to be if Shugborough were to continue at all, and it was the National Trust and then Staffordshire County Council that came to its rescue. Were it not for them much of the beauty seen here today would have faded, perhaps beyond repair, the costs of maintenance being too great a burden for the family to support. The house not only continues to exist but to improve year by year and it is no small wonder that so many come to see it – many again and again. When I see my children's faces as they wander around Shugborough Park Farm, I know that there is plenty here to replace my nostalgia for those days gone by.

Admiral Lord Anson (1697–1762), the founder of the Anson family fortunes; painted by Sir Joshua Reynolds, 1755 (Saloon)

CHAPTER ONE

ADMIRAL LORD ANSON

In order to understand the story of Shugborough it is best to begin not at the beginning but with the career of Admiral Lord Anson who raised the family to greatness in the mid-eighteenth century and made possible all that is seen there today.

George Anson was born on 23 February 1697, the second surviving son of William Anson of Shugborough by Isabella, daughter and co-heiress of Charles Carrier of Wirksworth, Derbyshire. Though Anson never owned the Shugborough estate, his endeavours made its creation possible, and the house and park are his best memorial – as his bachelor brother, Thomas, intended them to be.

George Anson has been hailed as the Father of the British Navy. The efficiency of his administration of the Admiralty and the strategic reforms which he instituted paved the way for the great sea victories of the Seven Years War and the consequent expansion of the British Empire. In particular, the captains and admirals whom he chose and promoted, and to whom he entrusted the command of the fleets, were all naval officers of genius: Boscawen, Brett, Dennis, Hawke, Howe, Keppel, Mostyn, Saumarez, Saunders, Warren. The last was Anson's second-in-command at the victory over de la Jonquière off Cape Finisterre in 1747, the first great British sea victory for fifty years and one which saw the whole of the enemy fleet either taken or destroyed. He said of Anson: 'I never wish to serve under a better chief', a measure of the Admiral's ability to instil enthusiasm and ideas into his subordinates.

The great improvements which Anson carried out while at the Admiralty, first under the Duke of Bedford and the Earl of Sandwich, then as First Sea Lord himself, included the improvement of the victualling of the navy and the sanitary arrangements on board, the coding of the Articles of War, the creation of a new standard uniform for naval officers, the institution of a permanent corps of the Royal Marines in 1755, the coppering of ships' bottoms which made them speedier, the standardising of ships, the building of a substantial number of new frigates, and the improvement of naval signal tactics. Perhaps he is best known, however, for his epic if gruesome four-year journey circumnavigating the world in 1740–4; he was only the second Englishman to achieve this feat, after Sir Francis Drake in the sixteenth century.

George Anson was early destined for the navy and, according to family tradition, was stirred by stories of the sea even as a small boy. He first joined as a volunteer aboard the *Ruby* under Captain John Chamberlain in 1712, aged only fourteen. He is next heard of on the *Monmouth*. In 1716, at the age of nineteen whilst serving in the frigate *Hampshire* in the Baltic, he received an acting order as a lieutenant from Admiral Sir John Norris, in command of a squadron sent to co-operate with a naval force of Russians, Danes and Dutch under Tsar Peter the Great against the Swedes, who were harrying neutral merchant shipping in the area. On his return to England, the commission was confirmed. The following year he was appointed to the *Montagu* under Sir George Byng and saw active service in the Mediterranean, taking part in the Battle of Passaro against the Spanish at the age of 21.

He obtained command of his first ship, the *Weasel*, a sloop, on 19 June 1722 and was successful in suppressing smuggling to the south coast of England from the ports of Holland. Two years later he was 'posted', sent out as a captain on the *Scarborough* to South Carolina where he was engaged in combating piracy against English merchant shipping. He served on and off at the South Carolina station until 1735, a total of eleven years. He proved himself an efficient officer and made many friends in colonial society, being modest and easy-tempered, benevolent, religious, fond of music and the bottle. A long letter from Mrs Hutchinson of South Carolina to her sister in London shows the favourable light in which Captain Anson was viewed by the settlers in the colony:

Mr. Anson is not one of those handsome men whose persons alone may recommend them to the generality of our sex, though they be destitute of sense, good nature or good manners; but, nevertheless, I think his person is what you would call very agreeable. He has good sense, good nature, is polite and well-bred; free from troublesome ceremoniousness. . . . He is generous without profusion, elegant without ostentation, and above all, of a most tender, humane disposition. At balls, plays, concerts etc. I have often the pleasure of seeing, and sometimes of conversing with, Mr. Anson, who I assure you is far from being an anchorite, though not what we call a modern pretty fellow,

because he is really so old-fashioned as to make some profession of religion . . . he is passionately fond of music. . . .

But I would convince you that all I have already said . . . is not merely panegyrical. I will give you an account of his faults too, as well as of his virtues. . . . In short, it is averred, that he loves his bottle and his friend so well, that he will not be very soon tired of their company, especially when they happened to be perfectly to his taste which is pretty nice as to both: moreover, if fame says true, he is very far from being a woman-hater, and that now and then his mistress may come in for a share of him.[1]

When war with Spain broke out again in 1739, following a period of drawn-out acrimony over the searching of British merchant ships, the government decided to dispatch a naval expedition against the richest and most distant Spanish possessions, to

Model of HMS *Centurion*, in which Anson sailed round the world

Sea-lion and lioness observed on the island of Juan Fernandez. This engraving was made for the popular account of Anson's voyage published after his return to Britain in 1744

try to cut off supplies of treasure from the New World. It was an ambitious and dangerous undertaking. Anson, with Captain Vernon, was put in charge of this great venture. On 9 December 1739, Anson was appointed to the *Centurion*, a ship of 60 guns and 400 men at the head of a squadron of five ships. The original aim was to attack Manila, but instead Anson was instructed to proceed to the South Seas to harass Spanish shipping, with the option of returning home via China if he wished.

The expedition lasted nearly four years, from 1740 to 1744, and was a remarkable personal triumph over every adversity and hardship. Some things went wrong from the start. Difficulty in manning the ships forced the Admiralty to recruit invalids and pensioners to make up the complement, most of whom were destined to die of scurvy and dysentery *en route*.

A powerful Spanish squadron under Pizarro was sent to intercept Anson's ships, but failed to find them and was broken up in bad weather off Cape Horn. Though Anson himself did not know at the time of this stroke of providence, and expected a Spanish attack at any moment, he sailed steadfastly towards Brazil via Madeira. It proved necessary to disembark at St Catherine, Brazil, to clean and re-fit the ships and to allow his sickly crew to recover on dry land with a diet of fresh meat, fruit and vegetables.

The squadron set sail in January 1741 for the journey round Cape Horn. Unfortunately the earlier delays meant that this perilous task had to be attempted at the worst season of the year. The squadron was buffeted continuously by terrible gales and snow storms for three months as they tried to round the Horn. The fitful suddenness of the squalls took men off guard, hurling them overboard or against large baulks of timber, breaking their bones. The freezing weather after the heat of the South American coast caused outbreaks of frost-bite. Most dispiriting was the lack of visible progress, with the ships being continually knocked off course and painfully having to retrace their steps. The squadron was scattered, never to be reunited as a whole. Outbreaks of scurvy became more and

The sweet pea brought back by Anson from Juan
Fernandez

helped the surviving men to recover. Anson planted
lettuces, carrots and other vegetables with seeds
brought from England; in return he took home the
beautiful blue sweet pea which is called after him.

Two of the other English ships, the *Tryal* and the
Gloucester, at last turned up, with crews even more
depleted by death and sickness than the *Centurion*.
The *Severn* and *Pearl* never appeared; it emerged
later that they had given up the attempt to round the
Horn and gone back to Brazil. Anson's three
remaining ships, which had sailed from England
with 961 men amongst them, were reduced to 335
when they left Juan Fernandez. Nevertheless, the
reduced crews were nursed back to health and
proved able to capture several small Spanish ships,
including the *Nuestra del Monte Carmel*. By this
stage, the *Tryal* was in such bad condition that
Anson was obliged to scuttle it and to transfer the
crew to one of the Spanish prize ships.

Still determined to carry out his instructions as far
as his reduced power allowed, Anson decided next
to attack the town of Parita on the coast of Santa Fé,
acting on intelligence he had acquired from the
crews of the captured Spanish ships. Lieutenant
Piercy Brett, his second-in-command, was appointed to lead a small land force of 58 men against the
town. They were rowed over at night, and, by
shouting, cheering and banging drums, they were
able to give the impression of a much larger force.
They surrounded the governor's house, captured
the fort and occupied the Customs House where the
treasure was stored, meeting with no opposition.
The surprised inhabitants and the Spanish governor
fled to the hills in their night clothes, to watch the
English from a safe distance. Anson sent a messenger
to the governor to come down to parley for the
town and to pay a ransom. He refused, so the place
was sacked and burnt, apart from two churches.
The treasure captured at Parita amounted to
£30,000, while shortly afterwards, Anson took
another Spanish ship with treasure worth £12,000.
The men, however, began to quarrel between those
who had gone ashore at Parita and those who had
stayed on the ships. The former expected to get the
lion's share of the prize money, while the latter
thought they should have equal pickings. Anson,
with typical fairness and generosity, solved this

more serious, confining the larger portion of the
crew to their hammocks while the number of deaths
increased daily. In April, 45 men died on the
Centurion, in May 80, and by mid-June the death toll
had risen to nearly 200 men. On 8 May 1741 the
Centurion reached the agreed rendezvous at Socotro
and cruised there for a fortnight awaiting the rest of
the squadron. But none of the other ships turned up
and, after the *Centurion* had been struck by light-
ning, Anson decided to go on to the island of Juan
Fernandez off the coast of Chile and anchor there.

Tents were erected on shore to which the sick
were carried in their hammocks, Anson himself
helping with this arduous work. Fresh fruit, vegetables, the meat of wild goats, sea-lions and fish

problem by declaring that everybody should have equal shares according to their rank, but that he would forgo his own captain's share and give it to those who had fought on land. This stopped the murmuring and restored general good spirits.

Anson's ambition was still to intercept and capture the annual Spanish galleon of treasure from Acapulco to Manila. But, fearing precisely that, the prize galleon did not sail at the prescribed date, so the English decided to cross the Pacific to China. Much to their surprise, the prisoners from Parita and the various prize ships, all of whom Anson had treated with exemplary fairness and humanity, were put ashore. The Spanish prize ships were scuttled and the *Gloucester* burnt. All the remaining crew were transferred to Anson's own ship, the *Centurion*, which alone made the journey.

Once again the voyage was dogged with bad weather and disagreeable circumstances, including a worse outbreak of scurvy. Desperate for fresh provisions, Anson hoisted Spanish colours retained from one of the prize ships and went ashore at the Spanish settlement of Guam on Tinian. There the sick were nursed back to health and the *Centurion* re-fitted for the next stage of the journey, setting off on 21 October 1742 for Macao. As the first British man-o'-war to visit China, the *Centurion* was an object of wonder. Anson sent a deputation to the Chinese viceroy at Canton to ask for provisions and, after some negotiation, he was provided with them. He was also able to recruit 23 new sailors, Dutch, Lascars and Indians.

Suitably refreshed and reinforced, he told his delighted crew that his aim was still to capture the

The capture of Parita on the coast of Santa Fé after a surprise attack by Anson's forces

The capture of the *Nuestra Señora de Covadonga*, the Spanish treasure galleon which made Anson's fortune; painted by John Cleveley in 1756 (Anson Room)

Acapulco treasure ship, the *Nuestra Señora de Cova-donga*. On 20 June 1743, they finally intercepted the Spanish galleon, commanded by General Dom Jeronimo de Montero. After a fierce skirmish lasting half an hour, Anson captured the ship. While the English suffered only three fatal casualties, the Spanish lost 67 men killed and 84 wounded. The value of the captured treasure amounted to no less than £400,000, and Anson's prize as captain made his fortune.

Once again, the *Centurion* sailed into Macao, this time with the captured Spanish galleon in tow. There the Spanish crew was liberated and the galleon sold to Dutch sailors for 6,000 dollars. This time, Anson found it more difficult to get provisions and was forced to visit the viceroy in person, leaving Piercy Brett in charge of the *Centurion*. Fate played into his hand, for while he was in Canton a serious fire broke out which his crew were able to bring under control. As a reward, Anson was given by the European merchants a magnificent Chinese export porcelain dinner service which is still at Shugborough, and the provisions for the home journey were soon forthcoming.

The *Centurion* set sail on 7 December 1743, reaching the Cape of Good Hope on 11 March. Anson rested there until April and enlisted a further 40 men before setting off for the north and home. They passed St Helena on 19 April and on 10 June reached the English Channel. Here the *Centurion* had a further stroke of luck; it sailed right through the middle of a hostile French fleet but, because of fog, was not recognised. Anson finally arrived at Spithead on 15 June 1744, after an absence of three years and nine months. A history of the eventful journey, published in 1748 by the chaplain of the *Centurion*, the Rev. Richard Walter, proved so popular that it went through fifteen editions.[2]

On 19 June George Anson was promoted to Rear-Admiral of the Blue in recognition of his signal service, but he turned down this offer because the Admiralty refused to accede to his request that his First Lieutenant, Piercy Brett, should be promoted to Captain. Such an act on Anson's part could have had a serious effect on his career. But a reshuffle in the government in December 1744 brought in the Duke of Bedford and the Earl of Sandwich as First and Second Lords of the Admiralty, and they selected Anson to serve on the Board. On 20 April 1745 he was appointed Vice-Admiral of the White, a two-step promotion ignoring the fact that he had turned down the intermediate rank.

The combination of Bedford, Sandwich and Anson at the Admiralty opened a new chapter in eighteenth-century naval history. After a period of laxity, even incompetence, new energy, determination and zeal for efficiency were brought to the navy. The dockyards were inspected, their administration overhauled, and negligence, waste and embezzlement stamped out. A system of similar inspections was established on a regular basis. New Articles of War were drawn up, old admirals were superannuated and improvements in ship design and construction introduced.

In 1747, during the War of the Austrian Succession, Anson once more went to sea, this time in the *Prince George* in command of a fine fleet against the French. His task was to protect English shipping in the Channel and to capture French privateers. On 3 May 1747, he caught the French fleet, commanded by Jonquière in *L'Invincible*, off Cape Finisterre and engaged it in battle. Approaching in

Anson led a deputation to the Chinese viceroy at Canton to get provisions for his beleaguered crew

The Battle of Cape Finisterre in 1747, when Anson defeated the French; by Samuel Scott (National Maritime Museum)

Commodore the Hon. Augustus Keppel, painted by Sir Joshua Reynolds in 1749 in the uniform Anson introduced to the Royal Navy (National Maritime Museum)

line order, he suddenly gave the signal for the English ships to break and to chase their French opposite numbers. The French, totally disconcerted by these new tactics, lost six out of ten men-o'-war, five armed Indiamen, 10,000 troops, their general and all the money and stores intended for their forces in Canada, valued at £2 million. Anson's victory crippled French naval power; the Marquis de la Jonquière is reputed to have said to Anson when surrendering his sword: 'Vous avez vaincu *L'Invincible* et *La Gloire* vous suit,' pointing to the ships of those names. The committee of the East India Company wrote jubilantly to the Lords of the Admiralty: 'The news from Anson will be the preservation of the East India Company'.[3] Anson himself was given a peerage, being created Lord Anson, Baron of Soberton in the County of Southampton on 13 June 1747, and promoted to Vice-Admiral of the Red on 15 July the same year.

Lord Anson then returned to his desk to continue work at the Admiralty. Another new innovation at this time was a standard uniform for officers, comprising a dark blue coat with white and gold collar, facings and cuffs. Formerly there had been no naval uniform, and many officers had worn old military red coats which they differentiated by adding black trimmings. There is an old story that the new uniform was based on the Duchess of Bedford's riding habit which had taken the King's fancy. But this, like many good stories, is apocryphal. The choice of uniform seems to have been Anson's. In a letter to Captain Philip Saumarez on 25 August 1747, Captain Keppel wrote: 'Tim Brett tells me you have made a uniform coat etc. after your own fancy; my Lord Anson is desirous that

many of us should make coats after our own tastes, and then that a choice should be made of one to be general, and if you will appear in it here, he says he will be answerable your taste will not be amongst the worst.'

On 12 February 1748, Lord Sandwich replaced the Duke of Bedford, who was indisposed with gout, as First Lord of the Admiralty. Sandwich and Anson made a good working team. They had much in common: Sandwich was able and intelligent, 'a scholar, a man of just observation, cultivated intellect and vigorous mind', and both had an interest

Lady Elizabeth Yorke
(d.1760), who married
Lord Anson in 1748;
studio of Thomas Hudson
(Saloon)

in music. Horace Walpole, however, was less enthusiastic and wrote in his waspish way: 'Lord Sandwich had been hoisted on the head of the Admiralty by the weight of the Duke of Bedford into whose affection he had worked himself by intrigues, cricket matches and acting plays'.[4] Walpole was hardly less mordant about Anson: 'Lord Anson was reserved and proud, and so ignorant of the world that Sir Charles Williams said he had been round it, but never in it. He had been strictly united with the Duke of Bedford and Lord Sandwich but, not having the same command of his ambition that he had of his other passions, he had not been able to refuse the offer of the Chancellor's daughter, nor the direction of the Admiralty.' Even

Walpole, however, allowed that Anson was 'generally expert in maritime details [and] selected with great care the best officers'.[5]

In 1748, Lord Anson married Elizabeth, the eldest daughter of Philip Yorke, 1st Earl of Hardwicke, Lord High Chancellor of England (whose seat at Wimpole Hall, Cambridgeshire, also now belongs to the National Trust). She too shared much in common with Anson, being gifted, indeed scholarly. They both subscribed to a number of new architectural and other books. She was, however, less reserved than her husband. Mrs Delany wrote in November 1749: 'She is a little coxcombical, and affects to be learned, which may sometimes put him out of countenance; but Lord Anson is a most

Allegorical portrait commemorating Sir Edward Hawke's victory at Quiberon Bay in 1759. Anson, then First Lord of the Admiralty, stands second from the right (Red Drawing Room)

generous goodnatured amiable man, and he deserved a wife of more dignity.'[6] From now on Lord Anson spent the greater part of his life at his town house in St James's Square, and his villa at Carshalton near London, interspersed with extended visits to his brother's country house at Shugborough, until he acquired his own enormous country house at Moor Park in Middlesex.

From 1748, Sandwich and Anson set about introducing a new class of frigate for cruising in wartime to replace the old 40-gun ships which were found to be too cramped. The new class of 36 guns proved very useful in the Seven Years War. In June 1751, Anson was promoted to First Lord of the Admiralty, a post he held with one short interruption until his death in 1762. He was also appointed Vice-Admiral of the United Kingdom, Master of Trinity House from 1752 to 1756 and a member of the Privy Council from March 1750. Using his dominant position to build up British naval power, he ensured that on the outbreak of the Seven Years War England had 130 ships of the line as opposed to the French 63.

The war at sea began ill with England's failure to relieve Minorca, followed by the unjust court martial of Admiral Byng who was held responsible for this failure; he was in due course shot on his own quarter-deck, in Voltaire's undying phrase 'pour encourager les autres'. This disaster caused the fall of the Ministry and with it Anson's removal from the Admiralty in November 1756, but he was back by July 1757, once more running things with his usual efficiency and zeal.

Perhaps Anson's greatest contribution was the promotion of a series of brilliant naval officers. Sir John Barrow wrote: 'Anson was remarkable for having brought forward such a number of fine officers, who figured as captains and admirals in the Seven Years' War. . . . His judgement was great, and he improved and gave a spur to the navy.'[7] The results were soon clear to all. In July 1758, Boscawen recaptured Louisburg at the mouth of the St Lawrence river in Canada and Sir Charles Saunders provided the naval back-up for Wolfe's conquest of Canada. In the Channel, Howe blockaded the French in their ports, and the following year, 1759, Sir Edward Hawke destroyed the French fleet at

Quiberon Bay, sinking or capturing seven ships and grounding the remainder for the rest of the war, thus dashing Choiseul's plan to invade England.

Anson's own last sea voyage was in command of the squadron of yachts that brought Princess Charlotte of Mecklenburg-Strelitz to England in July 1761 to marry King George III. At this time he was created Admiral and Commander-in-Chief of the Fleet. He died on 2 June 1762, four months before the Peace of Fontainebleau which triumphantly concluded the Seven Years War. He left the English navy at an unprecedented pitch of power and pre-eminence, with France and Spain seriously undermined as sea powers.

His death came suddenly, while walking in his garden at Moor Park. Neither he nor his brother had any children but at the time of his death a new patent was being prepared to create him a viscount with special remainder to the son of his sister Janette, George Adams of Orgreave in Staffordshire. In the event this did not materialise, but George Adams, who eventually inherited both his uncles' fortunes, took the name Anson and his son Thomas was in due course created Viscount Anson. In his will Admiral Anson left all his estate 'Real and Personal' to his brother Thomas, to his sister an annuity of £300 p.a. and to George Adams £500 p.a. 'for his life'.[8]

NOTES

1 Quoted in Sir John Barrow, *The Life of George, Lord Anson* (1839), pp.13–15.

2 Rev. Richard Walter, *Voyage Round The World 1740–44* (1748).

3 Walter Vernon Anson, *The Life of Admiral Lord Anson* (1912), pp.104, 105.

4 Quoted in Barrow, op. cit., p.151.

5 Horace Walpole, *Memoirs of the Last Years of George II*.

6 *Complete Peerage*.

7 Barrow, ibid., p.400.

8 PRO PROB 11/876 qr.230. Will of the Rt. Hon. George late Lord Anson Baron of Soberton, Co. Southampton.

CHAPTER TWO
THOMAS ANSON AND THE CREATION OF A SEAT

Thomas Anson, the Admiral's elder brother, was responsible for developing the old family seat at Shugborough into a fine park and substantial country house. He had inherited the estate from his father, William, in 1720 and was squire there for over fifty years until his death in 1773. He never married, devoting his energies to building, planting and collecting. When he succeeded, the property comprised a medium-sized house which fitted into the landscape of a riverside village, and about 90 acres of freehold land. His family were locally important but 'neither their place in society nor their house could be compared with that of the

Thomas Anson? (1695–1773), in the manner of John Vanderbank (Ante Room)

overlords of Shugborough, the Pagets of Beaudesert, or of the Ansons' neighbours whose houses were plainly visible from viewpoints in and near the village, the Astons of Tixall and the Chetwynds of Ingestre'.[1] Just as the Admiral transformed the economic and social position of the family, however, Thomas was able to transform the house into a mansion and the surrounding landscape into one of the finest Rococo park layouts in the country. Sir John Parnell wrote in his journal in 1769 that Shugborough 'in my opinion deserves to be accounted one of the finest Improvements in England . . . thro the whole is a great neatness, much taste, a turn to Roman splendour and avoiding mere lordly expense as much as any Place I have seen.'[2]

The house which had been built by Thomas's father, William Anson, in 1695 was a compact, brick, two-storeyed block which forms the nucleus, albeit much remodelled, of the existing house. During the Middle Ages, Shugborough had formed part of the Trent Valley estate of the Bishop of Lichfield, a village in the manor of Haywood, about halfway between his palace at Lichfield and his castle at Eccleshall. On this low-lying site at the confluence of the rivers Sow and Trent, a moated manor house was built for the Bishop. This, together with the greater part of the Trent Valley estate, was acquired in 1546 by William Paget, one of the 'new men' risen to power and riches in the service of Henry VIII. However, the Pagets developed as their family seat not the manor house at Shugborough, but the bishops' former hunting lodge at Beaudesert on Cannock Chase. Shugborough was sold by them to Thomas Whitby, who in turn sold it to Thomas Anson of Dunston, a successful lawyer, in 1624.

The property consisted of the medieval manor house and some 80 acres of land in the form of scattered fields there and across the River Trent at

Shugborough and the park from the east, showing Stuart's monuments, by Nicholas Dall, c.1768 (Swallow Passage)

Great Haywood. Between these fields and the house itself stood a substantial village of sixteen cottages along a village street running up from the Essex Bridge, a corn (later paper) mill near the bridge, another fulling mill with a large mill pond on the site approximately occupied now by Park Farm, and sixteen other cottages grouped along the roads and lanes leading towards Cannock Chase to the south and west of the house. Outside this central nucleus there were one or two further isolated cottages on the outskirts of the arable land. Most of these and the land around the village were copyholds held under manorial tenure from the Pagets of Beaudesert.

It is not clear whether the Ansons lived in the old manor house at Shugborough before the construction of the new house in 1695. But once resident, they gradually absorbed the rest of the village, buying the freeholds, leaseholds and copyholds of the other tenants of the manor of Haywood piecemeal as well as expanding outwards into the manorial waste on the slopes of Cannock Chase. An unusual, perhaps even unique, aspect of Thomas Anson's development of the park at Shugborough was that part of it, including the site of some of James 'Athenian' Stuart's more elaborate architectural monuments, was not freehold land at the time of his improvements, but amounted to little more than squatting on the manorial waste.[3] The Ansons started to expand their holding in the village at the time they built the new house, but it was not until about 1740 that Thomas Anson began to acquire additional property on a large scale at Shugborough. This suggests that he had already conceived a plan of development and embellishment of his estate even before his brother set out on the voyage of circumnavigation in the *Centurion*, which made the family fortunes.

Admiral Anson's success, however, transformed the scale of his brother's thinking and the years following his return in 1744 saw a great flurry of activity at Shugborough. In 1731, Thomas had obtained the lower mill near the Essex Bridge, together with its pool and stream, control of which formed the key to the early landscaping features at Shugborough. Between 1737 and 1740, he took formal possession of seven further pieces of copyhold property. By the time of the land tax return of 1741, he owned a quarter of the village and, throughout the next decade, he continued to

The Ruins at Shugborough, by Nicholas Dall, 1775 (Bust Parlour)

acquire further copyhold property. As he bought them up, he demolished the cottages on them. By this process, what had been a densely built-up village in front of the house was transformed piecemeal into open parkland. By the time of his death, Thomas Anson had gained control of the greater part of the former village of Shugborough and over a thousand acres of the slopes of Cannock Chase overlooking it, and had converted the area into a model landscape by planting trees and erecting ornamental buildings. The former mill pond was extended to make a small lake, embellished with a Chinese pagoda at one end and an ornamental cascade in the form of an open portico on top, or 'Palladian bridge', disguising a change of level in the middle. The stream which ran in front of the house was culverted and large sections of the old network of roads which criss-crossed the Shugborough plain were closed or diverted. New cottages were built for the displaced villagers at Haywood nearby.

The gardens and park as developed in these years must have been largely Thomas Anson's own brainchild, though involving a series of designers for different features. First came a Rococo layout with serpentine walks and water, shrubberies and lighthearted architecture, though later the park developed into the *locus classicus* of early neo-Classicism and the serious Greek Revival. The initial phase of the 1740s and '50s concentrated on the area to the north and west of the house and comprised a group of artificial ruins on the bank of the River Sow, reputedly constructed out of remaining stonework from the bishops' ancient manor house, and various *chinoiserie* structures recalling Admiral Anson's visit to Canton in 1743. The most important of these, happily still surviving, was the Chinese House, erected in the middle of a naturalised arm of the medieval moat adjoining the River Sow and approached by a pair of bridges. It was probably the first of Anson's garden buildings, put up in about 1747. Thomas Pennant (see page 32) states that it is 'a true pattern of the architecture of that nation, not a mongrel invention of British carpenters, taken in the country by the skilful pencil of Sir Piercy

Brett'.[4] Its purpose was partly to house the collection of Chinese porcelain, painted mirrors and other artefacts brought back to England by the Admiral, all of which were spared in the 1842 sale and removed for safe-keeping to the house itself in 1885. The exterior was painted pale blue and white with fret patterns, while the interior had a richly lacquered colour scheme of red, green, blue and gold. A long poem of 1767 about Shugborough, attributed to Anna Seward, 'the Swan of Lichfield', celebrated the delights of the Chinese temple:

Here mayst thou oft regale in Leric Bower,
Secure of Mandarins' despotic power . . .
Safe from their servile yoke their arts command
And Grecian domes erect in Freedom's Land.

Apart from the *chinoiserie* bridges, the other major Chinese monument at Shugborough was the timber pagoda which appears in views of the park by both Nicholas Thomas Dall and Moses Griffith. In a letter to the Admiral in November 1752, his wife announced that the skeleton of the pagoda was up 'and promises greatly'. It was situated at the south end of the lake facing the Temple of the Winds at the north end, but seems to have been swept away in a flood later in the century.

Because of the flat character of the landscape, Anson depended largely on water, trees and architectural elements to create the bones of his park. His plans received a further fillip when he inherited his brother's fortune in 1762. With ample funds now at

The Chinese House

The Arch of Hadrian, engraving from 'Athenian' Stuart's *The Antiquities of Athens* (1762)

his disposal, he turned to 'Athenian' Stuart to transmogrify the park into a three-dimensional version of illustrations from Stuart's book, *The Antiquities of Athens*, the first volume of which appeared in the same year. Solidly built of stone, Stuart's buildings mostly survive. The exception is the orangery or greenhouse, originally built in 1750, but reconstructed by Stuart in 1764 and demolished *c*.1855. It stood at right angles to the River Sow in front of the house facing over a bowling green, with a colonnaded façade to the south, and at the west end an alcove or apse with coffered semi-dome and a large architectural painting of the Temple of Minerva Polias (in Rome), carried out by N.T. Dall in oils so as to be 'safe from the effluvia of the orange trees'. As well as exotic plants, the greenhouse was intended to display part of Thomas Anson's collection of antique sculpture as well as two 'modern

statues' of Hymen and Narcissus. The 1767 poem paid poetic tribute to the building before it was embellished by Stuart:

Where the stately colonnade extends
Its pillar'd length, to shade the sculptured forms
Of Demigods or Heroes, and protect
From the cold northern blast each tender plant,
The fragrant progeny of milder climes.
Orange and lime, and cedars from the banks
Of Arno or Parthenope's soft shore,
There in fair order rang'd, stage above stage,
Rear to the lofty roof their green heads, crown'd
At once with flowers profuse and golden fruit,
A sylvan theatre . . .
Here while we breathe perfume, the ravish'd eye
Surveys the miracles of Grecian art.[5]

Anson began extending his landscape designs south and westwards from his house in the 1760s over what had been the village and manorial waste which he enclosed and planted with trees. Here he

(*Facing page*) The Arch of Hadrian at Shugborough

(*Above*) The Tower of
the Winds at
Shugborough,
showing the painted
frieze of the winds
with which it was
apparently once
decorated; engraving
after watercolour by
Moses Griffith

(*Right*) The Tower of
the Winds, engraving
from 'Athenian'
Stuart's *The Antiquities
of Athens* (1762)

erected the major Grecian monuments. The most prominent, and one of the first to be undertaken by Stuart for Anson, was the copy of the Arch of Hadrian at Athens, standing proudly on the highest point in the park. It was begun in 1761 but only completed in 1764, by which time it had acquired a new purpose, to commemorate Admiral and Lady Anson. The upper stage of the arch contains marble sarcophagi surmounted by busts of them, flanking a triumphal *aplustre* in the centre. *Aplustre* is the term used by Stuart for a naval trophy comprising the curved stern of a ship, together with its ornaments 'symbolic of the spoils of war'. These busts, the *aplustre*, together with the medallions representing Minerva and Neptune establishing naval discipline, were all the work of Peter Scheemakers, a sculptor much employed by Thomas Anson both at Shugborough and in London.

Hardly less ambitious than the Arch of Hadrian was the Tower of the Winds, erected at the opposite end of the lake to the pagoda. This is a remarkably accurate copy of the original as engraved in Volume I of Stuart's *The Antiquities of Athens*, even down to the duplicated entrance porches and the apsidal excrescence on the back containing the staircase. The only major difference is that the Shugborough version has windows in the sides; the original, being a sort of public clock tower, had blank walls with sundials. The Shugborough Temple was at first intended to carry sculpted reliefs of the winds in the frieze panels round the top of the walls. Strangely, they show on the Moses Griffith watercolour; possibly they were only painted in *trompe l'oeil*. The upstairs banqueting room was richly fitted with a 'domed and lozange-coffered ceiling after the manner of Nero's Pallace'[6], and finely carved joinery, chimney-piece and pier glasses all *en suite*. The lower room was originally a more simple interior, but embellished with the casts of centaurs, now in the Entrance Hall of the house, and a statue of Mercury.

Stuart had spent two years in Athens with Nicholas Revett, from March 1751 to the end of 1753, diligently surveying and making measured drawings of the major Classical ruins in the city. They were fortunate in being delayed on their way in Venice where Sir James Gray, the British Resi-

James 'Athenian' Stuart, the architect of the neo-Classical monuments in the park at Shugborough; miniature attributed to Philip Jean (National Portrait Gallery, London)

dent, was brother of the secretary of the Society of Dilettanti, established in 1732 for the encouragement of Greek Classical art. He was enthusiastic about their project and set in hand a subscription for financing it through the Society. Thomas Anson was a founder member and both he and Admiral Anson were subscribers to the first volume of *The Antiquities of Athens* when it came out in 1762. It was also through the Society that Stuart came to Anson's notice, beginning a fruitful architectural association which led to the design of a new town house in St James's Square as well as the buildings at Shugborough. A certain amount of correspondence between them survives, describing the progress of work and indicating a free and familiar relationship. On one occasion, in September 1766, Stuart complained of his treatment by Anson's servants: 'the insolence of your people is insupportable'.[7]

In some ways the prettiest and most interesting of the Stuart structures is the copy of the Choragic Monument of Lysicrates, the original of which, dating from the late fourth century BC, was found by Stuart embedded in the walls of a Capuchin monastery in Athens. Stuart explains in his book how it was then commonly called the 'Lanthorn of Demosthenes' and was supposed to have been built by the orator as a place of study and retirement. This is why the Shugborough monument was christened the 'Dark Lanthorn'. But Stuart discovered an inscription on the original saying that it was erected by Lysicrates of Kikyana as a memorial to the victory of the boys of the tribe of Akamantis in a dramatic contest. It is a cylindrical structure with attached Corinthian columns. From holes in the upper surface of the stone flower on top, and from Classical literature, Stuart deduced that it had been intended as a monumental plinth to support a bronze tripod. Tripods were associated from the earliest Classical times with wealth, honour, hospitality and victory. Homer's heroes frequently gave each other finely wrought tripods as gifts of honour or as prizes of victory in athletic contests. And Stuart observed that both Hesiod and Pindar mentioned tripods as prizes for literary or athletic achievements or as votive offerings to temples. On this basis, in *The Antiquities* he published a conjectural reconstruction of the tripod which he thought originally must have surmounted the top of the Monument of Lysicrates.

At Shugborough, Thomas Anson gave Stuart the chance to reconstruct the tripod in three dimensions, and in 1764 chose the site for it on a knoll in the park. The tripod posed great technical problems which were overcome by the joint efforts of the two leading Midlands industrialists of the age, Matthew Boulton of the Soho Works in Handsworth, Birmingham, and Josiah Wedgwood of Etruria, Stoke-on-Trent. The original idea was to make the tripod in bronze, and Boulton to cast the three supports in his foundry, but the bowl proved too difficult. At this point, Wedgwood stepped in and solved the problem. He tells the story in a letter to his partner, Thomas Bentley, in December 1770:

I forgot to tell you that Mr Boulton was making an immense large Tripod for Mr Anson to finish the top of Demosthenes Lanthorn building there from Mr. Stewarts design. The legs were cast & weigh'd about 5 cwt. but they (the workmen) stagger'd at the bowl, & did not know which way to set about it. A Council of the workmen was call'd & every method of performing this wonderfull work canvass'd over. They concluded by shaking their heads, & ended where they begun. I then could hold no longer but told them very gravely they were all wrong – they had totally mistaken their Talents & their metals. Such great works should not be attempted in Copper or Brass. They must call in some able Potter to their assistance, and the works might be completed. – Would you

The Lanthorn of Demosthenes, or Choragic Monument of Lysicrates, engraving from 'Athenian' Stuart's *The Antiquities of Athens* (1762)

Stuart's reconstruction of the tripod of the Lanthorn of Demosthenes

think it? they took me at my word & I have got a fine jobb upon my hands in consequence of a little harmless boasting. – Mr. Stewart said he knew Mr. Anson would glory in having the Arts of Soho, & Etruria united in his Trypod & that it would be a feather in our Caps which that Good Gentleman would delight in taking every opportunity to shew to our advantage. So the matter stands at present, but Mr. Boulton, Mr. Darwin & I are to dine with Mr. Anson on New-years day & shall then talk the matter over again.'[8]

The bowl was finished in April 1771 when the whole tripod was set up and gilded. This ingenious artefact long ago disappeared, and the present tripod on top of the 'Lanthorn' is a copy in fibreglass, part of the restoration of the park monuments carried out by the National Trust since their acquisition of the estate.

When first built, all these Grecian structures were more prominent in the landscape than they are now because the newly planted trees were small by comparison, exaggerating the scale of the architecture. This can be seen in the views by Dall and Griffith which hang in the house. The park itself was treated as a *ferme ornée* with ornamental animals including milk-white cattle and a flock of Corsican goats, not to mention Thomas Anson's sister-in-law, the Admiral's lady, and a bevy of other friends

dressed as shepherdesses. From the start, the park was an attraction visited by neighbours and travellers. As the 1767 poem put it:

Sneyds, Wolseleys, Chetwynds, Bagots, all
A swarm to fill your worship's hall . . .
. . . New scenes open, other fabrics rise.
Unusual forms! from climates far remote
By thy adventurous Race not unexplored,
Anson, whose indefatigable course
Proceeding, circled the terraqueous globe.[9]

There was also a serious agricultural purpose behind the improvements, especially the enclosures on Cannock Chase where Thomas Anson created sheep pastures and arable fields, as well as planting hundreds of acres of mixed trees.

Though Thomas Anson began his great programme of improvements in the park and gardens, he soon turned his mind to extending the house and work on both continued in tandem for the rest of his life. The Admiral's marriage in 1748 provided a spur, and all efforts were immediately concentrated on enlarging and improving the old house. The architect employed is not known for certain but, as Eileen Harris has demonstrated, there is a very sound case for attributing the work to Thomas Wright on stylistic grounds.[10] Ideas, even materials for the alterations, were contributed by different members of the family, including Jemima, Marchioness Grey, sister-in-law of Elizabeth, Admiral Anson's new wife; the introduction of Wright to

Corsican goat kept by Thomas Anson at Shugborough

the Ansons probably occurred through Lady Grey who already knew his work elsewhere. The first major alteration to the house was the addition of a pair of two-storeyed wings on either side of the seventeenth-century main block, connected to the old house by single-storey links. Each of the pavilions was given a domed semi-circular bow on the main (east) front.

When Philip Yorke and his wife visited Shugborough in August 1748, the two new wings had already been added. In the north wing they found 'a fine new room of 38 ft. by 24 ft. with a large bow window in the middle ornamented in Stucco, and with large Pictures of Architecture painted at Bologna'. This is now the dining-room, but was then the drawing-room. The large paintings on the walls, commissioned in Bologna, were later altered by Nicholas Thomas Dall, a Scandinavian, who was

brought to England by Thomas Anson and became successful as a scene painter at Covent Garden. The Shugborough architectural capriccios executed in tempera on thick coarse Italian canvas are a rare survival of Bibienaesque theatrical paintings (see p.59) though much cut about and altered. In 1762 the Yorkes also admired the stucco ceiling with its central rectangular panel, a copy of Guido Reni's *Aurora*, and gave the name of the stuccoist responsible, 'Vassalli'.[11]

This room provides strong evidence for the 1740s work at Shugborough, having almost certainly been designed by Thomas Wright. Eileen Harris has pointed out the parallels with his work elsewhere. The scrolling foliate frieze surrounding the room is repeated exactly in an alternative design for a room at Nuthall Temple, Nottinghamshire, and the medallions in the cove are very similar to those in

Bow window and wall-paintings by Nicholas Dall in the Dining Room

Aurora, stucco ceiling decoration by Vassalli after Guido Reni in the Dining Room

the Menagerie at Horton, Northamptonshire (both buildings designed by Wright).

The principal room in the south wing also happily still survives. This is the library. Lady Grey 'described it in September 1748 as a new addition to the house and thought it 'exceedingly odd and pretty'.[12] It was made by joining together two rooms, one in the old part, one in the new wing, by means of a deep segmental arch, flanked by little Ionic columns. The bookcases are fitted into arched recesses and both parts have attractive Rococo plaster ceilings with reliefs of Fame and Minerva, and medallions of philosophers and the arts and sciences, presumably also by Vassalli to Wright's design. In this room, Thomas Anson concentrated his fine collection of books on art, architecture, the classics and travel, nearly all unfortunately dispersed in the great sale of 1842. His copy of Winckelmann's *Lettre sur les découvertes à Herculaneum* (1764) is one of the few survivors from a collection which included a complete series of Piranesi's engravings of Rome.

Thomas Anson's other alterations to the house were later obliterated as part of the further re-modelling of Shugborough at the end of the eighteenth century by the 1st Viscount Anson and Samuel Wyatt, but it seems clear from contemporary descriptions that the whole house was redecorated, as well as enlarged, in the late 1740s. In May 1749, Lady Grey described the new dining-room in the centre of the west front. This took the form of a large projecting five-windowed bow, encircled by attached columns and crowned with a balustrade. It is shown in Dall's painting of the house from the west *c.*1769. This may not have been an entirely successful new addition. Lady Grey was critical of the 'ridiculous' appearance of 'that part of the poor old house which has come down for this modern new fangled to rise'.[13] The major works of alteration carried on into 1750. In the course of that year Lady Anson recorded 'several new ornaments and improvements added daily'. These included dressing-rooms hung with 'the very prettiest Indian papers of the Landskip kind with figures' supplied by one of the Admiral's subordinates, Captain

The west front showing Wright's alterations; detail of painting by Nicholas Dall (Verandah Room Passage)

The Library

Dennis, and the gallery (now the Ante Room to the Dining Room), fitted with an arched recess to receive a model of the *Centurion* given by the Admiral but sold in 1842 and now in the National Maritime Museum at Greenwich. To an extent, the house was developed as something of a museum devoted to the Admiral's nautical achievements. The entrance hall, for instance, was embellished with 'sea pieces and stucco' commemorating the Admiral's naval victories, an idea suggested by Lady Grey. Lady Anson reported: 'The Action of Cape Finisterre is already up and looks finely; the burning of Payta is to be over the chimney and the Actions between the Centurion and the Galleon and the Lyon and Elizabeth on each side of the door into the room you dined in, and two other actions of Captains of My Lord's in the war over the other doors; so that the whole will be a kind of history.'

Thomas Wright's final achievement at Shugborough may have been the mysterious shepherd's monument in the garden, a sort of Boetian temple containing a beautiful marble relief by Scheemakers after Poussin's well-known painting *Et in Arcadia ego*. The flanking rustic Doric columns and entablature may have been added by Stuart, but the monument itself, with a carved stone rustic surround, predates his work. Eileen Harris has convincingly attributed this to Wright on the strength of the striking resemblance between its 'strange rough-hewn arch' and a plate from Wright's *Six Original Designs for Arbours*, published in 1755.[14] The exact significance of the mysterious inscription 'D O.U.O.S.V.A.V.V. M' is not known. The separate terminals D.M. possibly stand for *Dis manibus (sacrum)* – 'sacred to the dead' – which would suggest that it is commemorative.

In about 1768, Anson carried out further major alterations to the house, adding an extra storey to the links in order to increase bedroom accommodation. This increased the convenience of the interior but spoilt the external composition. The alterations were probably the work of 'Athenian' Stuart who designed an unusual cresting for the parapet comprised of anthemion, or honeysuckle, and butting goats' heads, based on an engraving by Piranesi (dated 1765), in the *Trattato della Introduzione e del Progresso delle Belle Arti in Europa*.

The Shepherd's Monument

In addition to creating the gardens, park and farm at Shugborough and converting the house into a magnificent country seat, Thomas Anson also formed a large collection of Old Master paintings, antique sculpture, ancient and modern medals, books and engravings. The greater part of this assemblage was sold in 1842, but the sale catalogue gives a good idea of the range and quality of the collection and indicates how well it represented the toast of the Society of the Dilettanti: 'Greek *gusto* and Roman *vertu*'.

Not a great deal is known about Thomas Anson's education, but he was obviously a man of cultivated mind. As already indicated, he was a founder member of the Society of Dilettanti, through which he came into contact with James 'Athenian' Stuart. In 1724–5, he undertook an extended Grand Tour. In the mid-eighteenth century, Lichfield was something of a centre of intellectual life. Thomas Anson became Member of Parliament for the borough in 1747 and several of the local worthies were his close friends, including Dr Seward the divine, whose daughter Anna may have written the descriptive poem about Shugborough already quoted. Thomas

The east front of Shugborough, showing Stuart's alterations, and the Essex Bridge; engraving after watercolour by Moses Griffith

Pennant, traveller and naturalist, was another friend and included a long description of Shugborough in his *Journey from Chester*. Anson was also involved with some of the early industrialists. As well as Josiah Wedgwood and Matthew Boulton, he supported James Brindley, the engineer, one of whose new canals bordered Shugborough Park.

Thomas Anson formed his art collection, which comprised about a hundred items of sculpture and 120 paintings, as well as medals ancient and modern, when he was over sixty. Most of it was acquired in Italy between 1765 and 1771, through the agency of Sir John Dick, the British Consul in Leghorn and Joseph Nollekens, the sculptor who was then resident in Rome and earned his living by dealing in antique marbles. Dick was largely responsible for the acquisition of the paintings while Nollekens acquired the antique sculpture.[15] The list of lots in the 1842 sale catalogue is the best inventory of the collection and gives a tantalising impression of the contents of Shugborough at the end of the Georgian period.

The quality of Thomas Anson's collection was variable. The antique sculpture was heavily restored in the fashion of the time, and some of the paintings were strongly doctored too. A 'Guido Reni' for instance, still at Shugborough, is now described as 'school of Honthorst', the Guidoesque figure having been added prior to its sale to Anson in 1766. The 'Rembrandt' (sold in 1842) is now thought to be by Koninck.

The greatest portion of the sculpture and medals was bought *en masse* from Lefroy, a merchant at Leghorn who went bankrupt and sold his collection via Dick in 1766. He claimed that he had spent forty years in its accumulation and that it was 'the most valuable one there is in Europe'. It comprised the bulk of the medals, antique busts and statues which adorned Shugborough in Thomas Anson's time. Its acquisition proved especially useful as several of the marbles which Anson had tried to acquire through Nollekens in Rome, including a pair of marble candlebra from the Palazzo Barberini, were refused export licences by the papal government. Nollekens, however, did send home some busts and sarcophagi, plaster casts of objects in the papal museums, including the Capitoline centaurs (originally in the Tower of the Winds and now in the entrance hall), 'a most Excellent Statue of an Adonis which I am assured will be one of the finest Antique Statues ever seen in England', a pair of *cippolino* table tops from Scarpellino in the Campo Vaccino (still in the Red Drawing Room at Shugborough) and examples of his own work, notably the *Castor and*

Pollux (now in the Victoria and Albert Museum) which was sold for £320 in 1842, more than three times the price fetched by any of the pieces of antique sculpture.

Though some of Anson's swans turned out to be geese, this was not the case with all of them. Several landscapes he acquired in England, notably at Dr Richard Mead's sale in March 1754, proved to be of higher quality than the Italian purchases through Dick in Leghorn. Certainly, the Dutch landscapes by Van de Velde and Cuyp, and a Claude from Dr Mead's collection, all fetched high prices in the 1842 sale.[16]

Castor and Pollux, copy of a Classical sculpture commissioned by Thomas Anson from Joseph Nollekens

NOTES

1 F.B. Stitt, 'Shugborough: The End of a Village', *Collections For a History of Staffordshire*, Fourth Series, VI, (1970) p.100.

2 LSE Library, Coll. Misc. 38/1, 'Journal of Sir John Parnell, Bart'.

3 Stitt, op. cit. p.87.

4 Thomas Pennant, *Journey from Chester to London* (1782).

5 Christopher Hussey, 'Shugborough, Staffordshire', *Country Life*, 25 February 1954 *et seq.*

6 LSE Library, Parnell Diary (Coll. Misc. 38).

7 *Survey of London*, Vol XXIX, 1960, p.143.

8 Barlaston, Wedgwood Archives: Josiah Wedgwood to Thomas Bentley 24–26 December 1770; Wedgwood to Stuart 29 January 1771; 3 April 1771.

9 Quoted in Hussey, ibid.

10 Eileen Harris, 'A Flair for the Grandiose', *Country Life*, 2 September 1971, pp.546–8.

11 Bedfordshire Record Office, 'Philip Yorke's Journal', 1762.

12 Bedfordshire Record Office, Grey MSS; L30/9a/2/3.

13 Ibid., L30/9a/2/32.

14 Harris, op. cit. p.548.

15 Staffs. R.O., Anson MSS, D615/P(A)/2; P(5) 1/6, Thomas Anson's correspondence with Joseph Nollekens and Sir John Dick, 1765–71.

16 Sale Catalogue of the Contents of Shugborough, 1842; Preliminary MS copy in the William Salt Library, Stafford.

CHAPTER THREE

SHUGBOROUGH UNDER VISCOUNT ANSON

Thomas Anson II*, the son of George Adams Anson and great-nephew of Admiral Anson and his brother Thomas Anson, inherited Shugborough in 1789. He immediately set about a major reconstruction of the house and the park as well as adding several subsidiary estate buildings. The work was undertaken in two distinct phases – the first between 1790 and 1798 and the second between 1803 and 1806. The first phase was devoted entirely to remodelling and enlarging the house. The second phase, while it saw a further addition to the house, was chiefly occupied with the park and subsidiary buildings.

He chose as his architect Samuel Wyatt (1737–1807), a leading neo-Classical designer, elder brother of the more famous James Wyatt, and a man with strong Staffordshire connections. He had begun life as a carpenter, working for his father, a farmer, timber merchant and builder from Weeford, near Lichfield. His employment as clerk of works under Robert Adam at Kedleston, Derbyshire, in the 1760s amounted to a training in the most up-to-date Classical manner and enabled him to become an architect in his own right. He specialised in the design of medium-sized country houses and model farm buildings for which his elegant and restrained neo-Classical manner was well suited. Characteristic features of his houses are segmental bows and arches and a penchant for geometrical plan-making. The Classical detailing in his work is often derived from the most up-to-date Greek sources. A strong practical interest in building techniques led him to make extensive use of 'new' materials, such as Penrhyn slate and metal glazing bars.

Samuel Wyatt thought of himself as an engineer-

* In this chapter he will be referred to throughout as Viscount Anson to avoid confusion with his great-uncle, though he was not raised to the peerage until 1806.

architect rather than an artist-architect like his brother James. He had several friends among Midlands inventors and industrial pioneers, including Matthew Boulton, James Watt and Josiah Wedgwood. With his Staffordshire connections, he must have seemed the obvious architect for Thomas Anson to choose, and he had already done work for neighbouring estates, including Blithfield, Sandon and Tixall. The new wing at Tixall, now demolished, built to his design, was clearly visible from Thomas Anson's park. Wyatt was also connected with the recently dead 'Athenian' Stuart, having executed the carpentry contracts for him at Greenwich Hospital, Blithfield and possibly at Shugborough itself, for there are payments to a Wyatt in Stuart's accounts for work at the house in 1763–8.[1]

Viscount Anson was a prominent member of the group of Whig aristocrats – including Earl Spencer, the Dukes of Norfolk and Bedford and Lord Petre – who supported Charles James Fox. For many years MP for Lichfield, he was created Viscount Anson during Fox's brief period in office following the death of William Pitt in 1806. One of the most outspoken of Foxite Whigs was T. W. Coke of Holkham in Norfolk. He was to become Viscount Anson's father-in-law, for Anson married Anne Margaret Coke in 1794. The work that Samuel Wyatt had carried out for Coke at Holkham was to be an important influence on the scheme undertaken at Shugborough, particularly in the second phase of Viscount Anson's improvements after 1803.

The piecemeal eighteenth-century growth of Shugborough had resulted in a façade without much unity or dignity. In particular, Stuart's external alterations had created an unpleasant dichotomy between the high narrow central block and the low spreading wings. The purpose of the alterations planned by Viscount Anson with Samuel

Wyatt was to pull the house together as well as to increase the accommodation. Wyatt solved the latter problem by increasing the size of the wings. This made it possible to create a large drawing-room 46 feet long in the north wing and to enlarge many of the other rooms. In addition, he completely transformed the exterior, giving it a new neo-Classical simplicity and unity. His changes reveal a great deal about the architectural taste of the Foxite Whigs at the end of the eighteenth century. Externally, the wings and centre were brought into better relationship with each other by the removal of the balustraded parapet from the centre and the addition of one to the wings in place of Stuart's small-scale cresting. The principal innovation was to carry the cornice level of the wings right across the east front of the house in the architrave of a new portico. This was a vast octostyle* Ionic structure without a pediment which covered the whole width and lower two storeys of the centre block. It completely altered the proportions of the house by disguising the high narrow centre which became, at least from close up, simply a portico beneath an insignificant attic. Thus, with the minimum of alteration, the character of the façade was changed. Vertical emphasis gave way to a comfortable horizontal spread, typical of Samuel Wyatt's best buildings.

The external detailing of the house was also considerably simplified. For instance, the oddly placed pediment with Rococo carving on the east front was removed. The central arched windows on the ground floor of the bows were made square-headed, an angular bay window at the end of the north wing was demolished, and the heavy aedicules with attached columns in the links on both fronts were replaced by plain tripartite windows.[2] The old thick sash bars in the windows gave place to new, more slender ones of copper alloy in mahogany frames.[3] Thus everywhere thick and intricate details were pared away and replaced by those qualities of austerity and attenuation which are an inherent part of Samuel Wyatt's neo-Classical style.

Samuel Wyatt (standing on the right), with the Elder Brethren of Trinity House, by Gainsborough Dupont

* an eight-columned portico.

35

The east front, showing the portico added by Wyatt

The external transformation of Shugborough was completed by cladding the whole house (including the internal cellar walls) in a skin of slate, polished, painted and sanded to represent ashlar of mechanical smoothness and precision. The slating account, which included 'common slating' the roof and 'slate casing' the exterior walls and the interior of the cellars, as well as the eight columns of the portico, came to £2,295 17s 9½d, nearly half the cost of Viscount Anson's first phase of building, which totalled £5,539 13s 0d (excluding Wyatt's commission of £106 9s 0d and £420 for his 'designs of the alterations and additions, various drawings for the workmen' and travel expenses).[4] In resorting to the costly method of slate casing on this scale, Anson and Wyatt were probably influenced by the earlier failure of 'Athenian' Stuart, who had tried to stucco the exterior but, because of the damp situation of the house in low-lying land next to the river, had not been able to get it to adhere and set properly.[5]

Shugborough was a very large-scale example of Wyatt's faith in the constructional possibilities of slate, an enthusiasm derived from the fact that his younger brother, Benjamin, was the agent to Lord Penrhyn, whose vast quarry in north Wales started to export slate to the whole of Britain in the last decades of the eighteenth century.

The construction of the portico was particularly novel; this part of the slate cladding, moreover, has survived down to the present day. Each column consists of a wooden core with a slate covering formed of twenty-four flutings in beaded fillets, and the capitals are of Coade stone. The columns have been seen by some art historians as an exercise in 'primitive architecture', but in fact anything less rustic than these attenuated columns with their precise detailing would be hard to imagine. It is unlikely that the construction of the portico had any stylistic symbolism for Wyatt. Rather it was typical of his enterprise in the use of new materials and building methods at a time when the onward march of the Industrial Revolution was beginning to have an impact on building technology after a static period of some centuries.

Thomas Anson's remodelling of the interior of Shugborough was equally comprehensive. Only the Rococo library and drawing-room (the latter refurnished as a dining-room) were retained. Apart from increasing the accommodation, Samuel Wyatt successfully introduced variety into the plan, making a virtue of the differences in scale resulting from the cumulative development of the house. Square rooms were converted into circles or enlivened by apses. The transformation of the old entrance hall was particularly ingenious. There Wyatt introduced a ring of eight Siena marble scagliola columns made by Joseph Alcott.[6] As well as giving the room an ambiguously oval effect, this disguised the differing proportions of the doors.

The two finest interiors created by Wyatt at this time are the Great Drawing Room (now the Red Drawing Room) and the Bird Room. Both have excellent stucco ceilings and friezes by Joseph Rose II. The Red Drawing Room is Wyatt's grandest surviving interior. All its fittings are of the highest quality, particularly the white marble and ormolu chimney-piece supplied by Richard Westmacott. This is almost identical in design to those supplied by Wyatt for Livermere Park, Suffolk, and Trinity House in London at the same time. The handsome marble chimney-pieces in the other principal rooms were supplied by different sculptors – John Deval the younger, Samuel Adron, Charles Rossi, John Bacon the elder and Peter Mathias Vangelder.[7] The walls were hung with paper or fabric, mainly satin striped in fawn or salmon and silver from Messrs

The Red Drawing Room

37

The west front, with Samuel Wyatt's extended end pavilions and projecting central bow

Eckhardt and Co. of London.[8] Biagio Rebecca also did some unspecified painting, possibly the extension of the Dall paintings in the Dining Room to cover a pair of blocked-up doorways.[9]

In replanning the interior, Anson and Wyatt aimed at making the house more comfortable. They demolished the state bedroom and dressing-room opening off Thomas Wright's drawing-room and converted the latter into the Dining Room. They effected a division between the state rooms and family rooms similar to the arrangement at other country houses of this date, including Doddington and Tatton, both in Cheshire. The whole of the ground floor of the centre and north wing was given over to 'rooms of parade', intended for entertainment. In the south wing a completely self-contained series of smaller, comfortable private rooms was contrived for family occupation. These were conveniently close to the service wing and were provided with their own staircase and in-

dependent entrance directly from the stable forecourt. This division between the private family flat and the state rooms, a standard feature of several late Georgian house plans, is particularly obvious and clear-cut at Shugborough. It reflects the greater emphasis placed on comfort and privacy in that period, with the development of a more relaxed and intimate way of life by the English upper classes, which was the envy of the rest of Europe.

The second phase of Viscount Anson's improvements at Shugborough, between 1803 and 1806, saw a further addition to the house, reputedly in preparation for a visit by the Prince Regent. This involved extending what had been the dining-room in the centre of the west front to create a large new Saloon, 52 feet long. Internally this was a great improvement, providing a much-needed central place of assembly on axis with the entrance hall. Its architectural form was probably derived from James Wyatt's similar projecting axial saloon at Broome Park, Kent.[10] Externally, however, the new centre-piece was not an embellishment. It took the form of a narrow projecting wing rising the full height of the house and terminating in a flat bow. The west front at Shugborough is, as a result, an unsuccessful composition and must have been so even before the irritating twentieth-century alterations exacerbated its incoherence. The central projection breaks the unity of the front and its shape, with the flat bowed end and tall thin proportions, is unattractive. These proportions were, however, forced on Samuel Wyatt. He made some attempt to integrate the bow into the façade by linking it to the projecting side wings with trellised verandahs, a device that James had also used at Broome. Although pretty in themselves, these verandahs do not have a strong enough architectural character to resolve the incoherence of the façade. Some of Stuart's Piranesian cresting removed from the wings was reused along the top of these verandahs.

The interior of the new Saloon was austerely monumental, contrasting strongly with the pretty Grecian decoration in Wyatt's earlier rooms at Shugborough. It is a sign of the change in architectural style that occurred in England about 1800 and led to what is loosely termed 'Regency'. Elaborate stucco has been eliminated, and even the twin chimney-pieces are of the simplest rectilinear design. Of white marble and metal, these chimney-pieces are by Charles Rossi, one of two young craftsmen who contributed to this new phase of work at Shugborough and who were to become leaders in their respective fields. The other was the stuccoist Francis Bernasconi who made the capitals of the twelve columns in the Saloon. Bernasconi became the most successful stuccoist of his time and was extensively employed by King George IV, both

The Saloon

at Windsor Castle and Buckingham Palace in the 1820s. The columns are the room's principal feature. They are of 'yellow antique' scagliola provided by Joseph Alcott.[11] The capitals are of simplified Corinthian design derived from the Temple of the Winds at Athens, as can be seen in the porches of Stuart's copy in the park at Shugborough.

Viscount Anson's work in the park and on the estate at Shugborough is as interesting as his remodelling of the house. He was in the forefront of the intellectual and economic developments of the day, for he was putting into effect the precepts of the Utilitarian theorists who stressed that beauty should derive from usefulness, and that landowners should set an example in progressive agricultural techniques to the smaller farmers in their respective counties by developing their demesnes as 'schools of agriculture'.

In the late eighteenth century, Staffordshire was as much in the vanguard of agricultural development as of industry. Lord Talbot's model farm of 1,600 acres at Ingestre, Lord Harrowby's at Sandon with buildings designed by Samuel Wyatt, Lord Bradford's at Weston with its great Palladian barn,

Sir John Wrottesley's at Wrottesley, and Sir George Pigot's of 1,200 acres at Patshull were among the best-run agricultural enterprises in England. But the Park Farm at Shugborough was intended to exceed all others in the county in scale and in the excellence of its buildings.

From 1795 onwards, Viscount Anson totally remodelled the Shugborough demesne with the intention of adapting a purely ornamental landscape to the needs of farming in the great age of English agricultural improvement. He embarked on this work with a ruthlessness which made contemporaries gasp with admiration. The line of the main Stafford–Lichfield road was diverted across Cannock Chase. An alternative channel was dug for the River Sow and a new bridge built half a mile upstream from the old, which was in turn demolished. The remnants of the village, clustering near the Tower of the Winds, were swept away and replaced by new cottages at Great Haywood.[12]

The immediate impetus for this energetic onslaught was the Great Flood of 1795, when the river burst its banks and ruined much of the original Rococo park layout, sweeping away such structures

The Lichfield Lodge

Anson crest and coat of arms on the Stafford Lodge

as the Chinese Pagoda in the process. John Webb, the Staffordshire rival to Repton, was called in to relandscape the grounds and was paid £9,541 3s 9¾d for his work at Shugborough between 1795 and 1805.[13] The concomitant new estate buildings were designed by Samuel Wyatt between 1800 and 1806.

The expansion of the park entailed building new drives and lodges. The two principal sets at the Lichfield and Stafford entrances are the finest in the county and are identical in appearance. In fact, only the Lichfield Lodge was built in Samuel Wyatt's own lifetime; the Stafford Lodge was erected to his design nearly twenty years after its twin. The Lichfield Lodge was originally situated at Great Haywood, but was later moved to its present site on the south-west side of the park when the London & North Western Railway drove the main line north through the estate.

Each gateway consists of twin cubic lodges with Tuscan columns *in antis** flanking recessed centres. This is a common Wyatt motif but is handled here with exceptional crispness. The particularly hand-

* recessed in plane of building.

† without columns or a visible order.

some effect is partly a matter of excellent proportions and partly due to the monolithic smoothness of the ashlar masonry, enhanced by niches scooped out of the corners and cameo-like medallions of Coade stone containing the Anson crest and arms. These were modelled by Charles Rossi, as were the Anson crests used as finials on top of the gate-piers. All the ironwork of the gates with 'ring friezes, halberd head spikes and strong-framed ornamental pilasters' was executed by John Mackell, a London smith much employed by the Wyatts.[14]

The displaced villagers were rehoused in model cottages forming two neat neo-Classical layouts. One group of twelve was arranged as a symmetrical approach to the Essex Bridge (and the original site of the Lichfield Lodge, now replaced by a railway arch). They form a pair of low two-storeyed terraces flanking the road. Each side is punctuated by one higher cottage with a Tuscan porch. The other cottage doors are astylar† and simply pedimented.

This small-scale monumental layout still exists, but Samuel Wyatt's other group at Great Haywood was regrettably demolished in about 1965. Known as the Ring, it formed sixteen cottages with a communal bake-oven in the centre of the inner yard. It was a good example of Samuel Wyatt's interest in pure geometrical composition, reminiscent on a simpler scale of contemporary French utopian visions of housing the people in buildings of extreme neo-Classical fantasy.

Another geometrical composition, which happily survives, is a little cottage in Stafford Wood probably intended for a woodsman. It is a two-

Wyatt's model cottages at Great Haywood

storeyed octagon with an hexagonal rear extension giving it, when seen side-on, a very curious appearance. Like the grander cottages at Great Haywood, it has a pedimented porch with baseless Tuscan columns, an order always used by Samuel Wyatt for subsidiary estate buildings, following Palladian precept.

The principal new building undertaken at Shugborough at this time was, however, the new Park Farm, sited within a stone's throw of Stuart's Temple of the Winds and significantly closer to the main house than the kitchen garden. In Viscount Anson's lifetime the farm was the heart of activity on the estate. It was undertaken on a scale in obvious emulation of Holkham, where Lord Anson's father-in-law, 'Coke of Norfolk', was completing his famous farm improvements. Anson married T. W. Coke's daughter Anne Margaret in the very year that he began his work on the estate at Shugborough, which must be more than a coincidence.

The pattern-book farm layout consists of a quadrangle with the farm steward's house on the side opposite the entrance and two long flanking ranges, one containing the stables and cattle sheds, the other a brew-house and a water-powered mill for the use of the family and farm and 'in which corn is ground for the neighbouring poor *gratis*'. The

waterwheel was restored in 1987. In the centre of the yard was 'a very complete hoggery built of large stones set edge-wise and covered with slate and a cold bath supplied by the mill stream for giving an occasional washing to the pigs'.[15] But this has since disappeared.

A further complex of farm buildings was situated about half a mile away at White Barn, containing the barns and the threshing machine, which was also worked by water power. This machine was the most modern of its kind, the first stationary threshing machine in Staffordshire. The example set by it was not followed until 1836 when water power was again used to drive a threshing machine at the Littleton estate on Cannock Chase.[16] The White Barn complex had served as the buildings for the home farm created by Thomas Anson on the slopes of Cannock Chase before the new Park Farm was built on the site of part of the old village. White Barn, too, was substantially remodelled by Wyatt, who added the projecting wings with lunette windows in order to give it more architectural presence.

The dairy was also a separate establishment, contrived in the ground floor of the Tower of the Winds. Samuel Wyatt prepared a wooden model for this conversion in 1803, and the work was

White Barn Farm

executed on a lavish scale. The walls were lined with Derbyshire alabaster 'worked into mouldings, arches, bevils and flatt slabs' by Richard Brown of Derby.[17]

The room was given a faintly ambiguous shape by the introduction of shallow-arched alcoves on all eight sides supporting a circular cornice, whereas the black marble skirting was octagonal. This is a good example of Samuel Wyatt's finesse in the contriving of subtle spatial effects. The dairy pots provided by Wedgwood were in the Egyptian style, but they have long been removed to the house for safe-keeping. The adaptation of the Tower of the Winds into a dairy is symptomatic of this whole phase in the development of Shugborough. The conversion of a purely decorative building into something more practical exemplifies the utilitarianism motivating Anson's improvements.

In his day, the Park Farm consisted of 2,000 acres of which 300 acres were barley, 100 acres turnips and 250 acres hay, in addition to large areas of wheat and grazing. The livestock comprised 100 head of cattle (including 30 dairy cows), 30 draught horses, 17 oxen and 1,700 Southdown sheep of the same breed as at Holkham. The labour-force under the farm steward, Mr Wheelock, included the mill-manager, 2 farm servants and 22 labourers. Extra hands were hired at harvest time and for special work, such as underdraining the fields. The wages of the labourers were 10s a week, in addition to which they received a generous beer allowance, free ale in harvest time and free dinners from time to time.

On an even grander scale than the Home Farm was the walled kitchen garden laid out in 1805–6. William Pitt gives a detailed description in 1817:

A kitchen garden of several acres is walled and subdivided; the walls well stocked with the choicest fruit trees, with very extensive ranges of hot-houses, in which the pineapple, the grape, the peach, the fig and other varieties of hot-house fruits, flowers and plants, are cultivated in the highest perfection. One of the hot-houses is heated with steam, in which melons and cucumbers are produced in perfection at all seasons. These gardens are a kind of Academy for the study of Horticulture, in which young men enter themselves to assist without pay, for the purpose of improving themselves, and gaining knowledge in the art.[18]

Now used for other purposes, the high brick walls and general layout survive; they are similar to Samuel Wyatt's kitchen garden at Holkham designed for T. W. Coke.

Altogether the farm was run on the firm but philanthropic lines typical of estate management among the Foxite Whigs. It was an approach which foreshadowed the policies of the more enlightened Victorian landowners. For this reason Lord Anson's estate improvements are as interesting from the social point of view as they are from the architectural.

NOTES

1 Staffs. R.O., Anson MSS, D615/E(H)1/2. Stuart's accounts 1763–8.

2 Shugborough, watercolours by Moses Griffith *c*.1780.

3 Staffs. R.O., D616/E(H)/2/5, Wyatt's account 1792–6.

4 Ibid., D615/E(H)2/1,2. Wyatt's account 1790–6 and 1794.

5 G. Beard, *Georgian Craftsmen* (1966), p.73.

6 Staffs. R.O., D615/E(H)2/4. He was paid £859 8s 10d for them.

7 Ibid., D615/E(H)2/4.

8 Ibid., D615/E(H)2/3,6.

9 Ibid., D615/E(H)2/4.

10 Built in 1778 for Sir Henry Oxenden (Howard Colvin, *A Biographical Dictionary of British Architects*, p.947). The resemblance is made clear in a sketch plan among William Drake's drawings (Bucks. R.O., D/DR/5/52).

11 Staffs. R.O. D615/E(H)2/3, Building Account 1804–6.

12 F. B. Stitt, 'Shugborough: The End of a Village', *Collections for a History of Staffordshire*, Fourth Series, VI, (1970) p.100.

13 Staffs. R.O., Anson MSS, D615/E(H)2/6. Accounts 1793–1813.

14 Ibid.

15 W. Pitt, *Topographical History of Staffordshire*, II (1817), pp.90–1.

16 J. E. C. Peters, *Development of Farm Buildings in Western Lowland Staffordshire* (1969), pp.88, 102.

17 Staffs. R.O., Anson MSS, D615/E(H)2/6. Accounts 1793–1813.

18 W. Pitt, ibid.

Thomas, 1st Earl of Lichfield (1795–1854), by or after Thomas Phillips (Ante Room)

CHAPTER FOUR
THE GREAT SALE AND REVIVAL

The 1st Viscount Anson died in 1818 and was succeeded by his son, Thomas William, as 2nd Viscount. He in turn was created Earl of Lichfield in the Coronation Honours of King William IV in 1831. The personal extravagance of the new Earl was to make serious inroads into the family fortune and to lead to the sale of Thomas Anson's library and collections of antique sculpture and Old Master paintings. On his father's death he inherited, according to the *Gentleman's Magazine*, 'a clear and unencumbered estate of £70,000 p.a.'. This must have been an exaggeration, but nevertheless it is clear that he started out with a large fortune which makes it all the more extraordinary that he got into such serious financial difficulties. Thomas Greville in his memoirs described him as 'a fine fellow, with an excellent disposition, liberal, hospitable, frank and gay, quick and intelligent, without cultivation, extravagant and imprudent, with considerable aptitude for business; between spending and speculating he has half ruined a noble estate'.[1]

A keen Whig, he played an active role in contemporary political life; during his tenure as Postmaster General from 1835–41 the Penny Post was introduced. He was a particular friend of Lord Melbourne, the Prime Minister, and organised the meeting in the library of his London house which secured the support of the Irish MPs for the Whigs, thus enabling Melbourne to form a government in 1835. This agreement is still known as the Lichfield House Compact.

The causes of his financial difficulties, apart from general extravagance, seem to have been threefold: political expenses, buying land, and speculations on the turf. The Ansons were a Whig family in a county where many of the landed gentry and prosperous townspeople were traditionally Tory. As part of their new role as landed magnates in the eighteenth century, the Ansons had built up their political influence in the county, as well as establishing Shugborough as a leading country house. The main object of their political ambitions was the control of the two MPs returned by Lichfield, a borough with a complicated franchise and, until the middle of the eighteenth century, a strong independent (Tory) party. Admiral Anson and his elder brother Thomas had joined with the Gowers of Trentham in an attempt to control both of the borough's seats. This struggle had been particularly expensive and bitter because the Gowers, originally Tories, had changed colours and become Whigs at that time, making them personally unpopular with their neighbours. The first Thomas Anson of Shugborough was called by Wedgwood 'the founder of the Whig party in Staffordshire', though it was his brother, the Admiral's fortune which financed the Anson parliamentary interest in Lichfield and their attempt to turn it into a Whig pocket borough. The 'honest interest' represented by the magistrates and freemen of Lichfield and many of the neighbouring country gentlemen, who had the right to vote, put up a determined fight against the Whig upstarts as they saw them. For instance, Dr Johnson's dislike of the Ansons was coloured by this political background.

The franchise of the borough of Lichfield was unusually complicated, even by the standards of English parliamentary boroughs before the 1832 Reform Bill. In 1718 the House of Commons had determined that in Lichfield the right of election was 'in the bailiffs, magistrates, freeholders of 40s p.a. and all that hold by burgage tenure, and in such freemen only of the said city as are enrolled, paying scot and lot there'. In the 1747 election Leveson Gower and Thomas Anson opposed the sitting Tory members, George Venables and Sir Lister Motte, and managed to defeat them by a handful of votes each. This victory was ruinously expensive

A Shooting Party at Ranton Abbey, by Sir Francis Grant, 1840 (Verandah Room Passage)

and is said to have cost Anson and Gower £20,000 between them in buying votes and huge 'expenses' to alehouse keepers. From then on, however, the Ansons became sitting members for Lichfield. In order to reduce the cost of future elections, they set about buying the burgage properties, which carried a right to vote, in Lichfield. This was a securer way of controlling the electorate than indiscriminate bribery. It proved successful, and after 1761 the only other contested election in Lichfield during the eighteenth century took place in 1799. The Ansons and Gowers controlled a seat each, nominating the MPs.[2] The acquisition of property in the town was obviously the best long-term policy to control the borough, but Lichfield's complex franchise meant that the dominant political interest could never rely entirely on its control of voting property. Con-siderable additional expenditure on bribes and entertainment was necessary on the occasion of each individual election. This proved a constant financial drain on the Anson purse up to the Great Reform Bill of 1832 and beyond.

The second great source of the 1st Earl's expen-diture lay in buying land, not around Shugborough, but elsewhere in Staffordshire. At Shugborough, the estate had been built up to its logical extent by Thomas Anson and the 1st Viscount, but it formed only the nucleus of the family holdings in Stafford-shire; there were also scattered properties in the east and west of the county. These the 1st Earl expanded to make more coherent and easily manageable properties, consolidating small landholdings into full-scale estates. In this, as in much else, he was greatly influenced by his grandfather, T. W. Coke at Holkham. Coke of Norfolk had spent a fortune in his lifetime consolidating his landholding around Holkham by buying up outlying properties and even whole neighbouring estates. This was partly in the interests of improved agriculture but also of sport. The early nineteenth century was the first great age of English shooting, with many leading landowners vying with each other in the creation of preserves, improving their coverts and outdoing each other in the size of the bags produced by their estates. The modern shoot, in the form of pre-arranged drives, with the birds driven by beaters from game coverts over static lines of guns, was invented at Holkham.[3]

Coke's achievements and interests had great influence on two successive generations of Ansons. Whereas in the late eighteenth and early nineteenth century the 1st Viscount had been much influenced by the improved agriculture at Holkham, for the 1st Earl it was his grandfather's sporting achievement that was the dominant influence. He concentrated on the Ranton Abbey estate to the west of Stafford. The house there had been bought by the 1st Viscount, but the 1st Earl greatly expanded the property, bought more land, planted coverts and spent large sums of money in making it into one of the finest sporting estates in the country. There he held a series of great shooting parties throughout the 1830s and made it into a centre of Whig sporting hospitality. George III's son, the Duke of Sussex,

came every year for a period of ten years, and Ranton Abbey was visited by the young Princess Victoria in 1832, as part of her first grown-up itinerary of English country houses. In the Verandah Room Passage at Shugborough hangs a famous painting by Sir Francis Grant, *A Shooting Party at Ranton Abbey*, painted there in 1840. Grant himself often shot with the Lichfields at Ranton, and his painting includes the 1st Earl of Lichfield, Lord Melbourne, then the Prime Minister, Lord Sefton and the Earl of Uxbridge.[4]

Both in the country and at his London home in St James's Square, the 1st Earl maintained an extravagant social life. In the 1820s he bought the Atherstone Hunt in Warwickshire, which was known for many years as the Anson Hunt. This cost him about £3,000 a year to run, in addition to such incidental expenses as renting a house at Atherstone every winter for the hunting season. He gave this up in 1830 when he became Master of the Royal Buck Hounds at Windsor. That too involved him in considerable expense, including the renting of a house, Fern Hill, in Windsor Great Park.

Against this general background of extravagance, the immediate cause of his financial collapse was his addiction to the turf. He owned a racing stable at Newmarket jointly with his brother, George, and a

Lord Anson's Hunt, by William Webb, 1827 (Red Drawing Room)

rich friend, Lord George Bentinck, brother of the Duke of Portland. Pictures of many of his horses hang at Shugborough. In 1836, the 1st Earl and Lord George Bentinck won the St Leger at Doncaster with *Elis*, a horse which had been transported from Lord George's stable at Goodwood, Sussex, in what must have been the first purpose-built horse box. This was a large ventilated wooden conveyance drawn by six posthorses with outriders. It formed something of a procession and the journey was broken at Lichfield where the horse galloped round the course.

A strong Anson connection with the Lichfield Race Course had been begun in the late eighteenth century by George Adams Anson and his son, the 1st Viscount. The 1st Earl continued this and held the Anson Hunt Races there every year. As well as being a breeder and trainer of horses, he was also a keen better. The sporting writer 'Nimrod' described him as a noble sportsman and a high better. The financial crisis of 1841–2 was sparked off by an action brought by a London lawyer against the Earl in person for £20,000. This lawyer was also, it appears, a bookie on the side. So the £20,000 owing to him was almost certainly the 1st Earl's racing expenses and betting debts. The estate was already mortgaged to its maximum, so no further money

could be raised that way. Debts had been accumulating since around 1820. At first, comparatively small loans had been raised locally from a number of different people through an attorney in Stafford. In 1838, all these debts were consolidated into one large mortgage of £600,000 with the Provident Assurance Company. The estate was to be saddled with this heavy interest liability until the 1880s.[5]

The only means of raising the £20,000 which Lord Lichfield needed to pay his personal debt was to sell the contents of his London house and Shugborough in 1842. The former took seven days and the latter fourteen. 'The interest increases as the sale proceeds', a newspaper reported. 'Several gentlemen of known judgment in the Fine Arts came down to Shugborough by the mail train on Sunday and the celebrated Italian collector Signor Basseggio arrived on purpose to make a selection from the antique sculpture.' He also bought paintings, being shown in the annotated copy of the sale catalogue to have spent £325 on the Claude landscape which Thomas Anson had bought from Dr Richard Mead's sale in 1754. Interest in the sale was international. As well as 'Signor Basseggio', purchases were made by a Dutchman who acquired the Rembrandt *Head of a Young Man*. The lion's share was bought, however, by the antique dealers of Wardour Street and Soho, then the centre of the London art trade.[6]

From a manuscript copy of the sale catalogue preserved in the William Salt Library at Stafford, it is clear that the original intention was to sell nearly everything. But by the time the catalogue was printed there had been a change of heart and all the family portraits and objects connected with Admiral Anson, including the contents of the Chinese House with its rare oriental porcelain and mirror paintings, had been withdrawn from the sale. The family silver, too, was retained. Of the total of £18,339 18s 11d realised by the Shugborough sale, lots worth £5,093 were bought in by the family, largely by the Earl's wife Lady Lichfield. She bought the furniture of the principal rooms, including the sets of seat furniture and pier tables in the drawing-rooms and Saloon. Fixtures like Dall's paintings in the Dining Room were not included in the sale. Nevertheless, all the furniture in the

Elis was trained by the 1st Earl and won the 1836 St Leger; painted by J. F. Herring (Verandah Room)

secondary rooms and thirty principal bedrooms, including the magnificent bed in the state bedroom, was lost forever. The principal victims, however, were (apart from the 10,000 bottles in the Wine Cellar) Thomas Anson's collections of sculpture, paintings and choice books. These were dispersed almost *in toto*. Today, only one book, three or four paintings in the drawing-rooms and on the staircase and one or two pieces of sculpture in the entrance hall survive to recall the discriminating taste in art of a founder-member of the Society of Dilettanti.

Following the sale, Shugborough was shut up with only the gardener living there as a caretaker. There were no live-in servants and all the former staff were pensioned off and moved out to cottages on the estate. The property was left ticking over on a shoestring, with the home farm let to a tenant farmer. Lord and Lady Lichfield went abroad to economise, returning from France in 1847. Tenants' parties were held to welcome them home, but otherwise they lived quietly thereafter, more at Ranton than at Shugborough, until Lord Lichfield's death in 1854 at the age of 58. His wife outlived him by another twenty years or so, dying in 1879. She had a reputation for being somewhat formidable. As an old lady she was described as 'still very handsome, pale, with dark hair, but had a stateliness of manner which was somewhat alarming to a raw youth'.[7]

The 1st Earl was succeeded by his son, Thomas George. The 2nd Earl had worked in the Foreign Office as a précis-writer from 1846, but on his parents' return to England gave that up and stood as MP for Lichfield, the last member of the family to do so after an almost uninterrupted run in the seat of nearly one hundred years. He was Liberal MP for Lichfield from 1847 until he inherited the title and moved to the Lords in 1854. The following year he married Harriet Georgiana Louisa, the eldest daughter of the 1st Duke of Abercorn and grand-daughter of the 6th Duke of Bedford. All seven of the Abercorn daughters married peers and formed a characteristic inner group within the mid-Victorian peerage – earnest, liberal, devoted to good works and not uncultivated. They all remained admirers and patrons of the artist Edwin Landseer, a close friend of the Russell family, and as a result several of

Landseer's drawings are now preserved at Shugborough. Lord Lichfield himself took a keen interest in prison reform and was an active worker in the movement for the establishment of reformatories with an emphasis on the reclamation rather than punishment of prisoners. He was the first chairman of the Society for the Reformation of Juvenile Offenders.

The first task of the young married couple was to refurbish and refurnish Shugborough, which had been largely empty for twelve years. Lichfield House in St James's Square, which had been let since 1842, was put on the market and sold for £12,750 to the Clerical, Medical and General Life Insurance Society (which still owns the building, and has maintained it well).[8] This produced some money to spend on Shugborough. The 2nd Earl did little to reduce the mortgage on the estate which remained

Louisa, Duchess of Abercorn and her daughter, Lady Harriet Hamilton, by Sir Edwin Landseer, 1834 (State Sitting Room). Lady Harriet married the 2nd Earl of Lichfield in 1855

at £600,000 until 1880. The interest on this, however, was bearable thanks to mid-Victorian prosperity and an agricultural boom that ran from 1850 to 1870. The home farm was taken back in hand under the direction of Mr McMeeken, the farm steward. Whereas it had occupied the entire Shugborough estate of 2,000 acres in Viscount Anson's time, it was now 350 to 400 acres, with the rest of the property let to tenants. At the home farm, 150 acres were under cultivation and the remainder was pasture, the emphasis being on milk and beef production with a large herd of pure-bred Shorthorn cows in place of Viscount Anson's famous Staffordshire Longhorns. Examples of both breeds can be seen today at Park Farm, which is run as a farm museum by the County Council.

When it came to refurbishing the house, Lord Lichfield relied on one of the leading London decorating firms of the day, Morant & Boyd. They supplied new furniture for the bedrooms, redecorated the main rooms, providing new carpets and curtains and even pictures. A copy of the pendant to the Zuccarelli on a curved canvas in the Blue Drawing Room, to replace the original sold in

1842, was provided, though the name of the artist is not known. Some of their work survives at Shugborough today, including the red plush upholstery on the Charles Smith chairs and sofas in the Saloon and the hangings and the carpet in the State Bedroom (recently rewoven to the original design).[9] The 2nd Earl also bought a lot of excellent French eighteenth-century furniture to make good his father's depredations.

Two of the 1st Earl's children earned posthumous fame. Augustus, his third son, had a distinguished military career with active service in the Crimea and India. Though mild-mannered, he is known to have been involved in hand-to-hand combat on 37 different occasions, and in all but three cases, he killed his opponent. He was a Lieutenant-Colonel in the 8th Hussars and won one of the earliest VCs, in South India during the Mutiny. The Anson Memorial Sword at Sandhurst is called after him.

Lady Louisa Mary Anne, the 1st Earl's eldest daughter, also gained a degree of immortality as the possible origin of the word 'loo' as a nickname for a lavatory. Steven Runciman tells the story:

The Staffordshire Longhorn breed championed by Viscount Anson

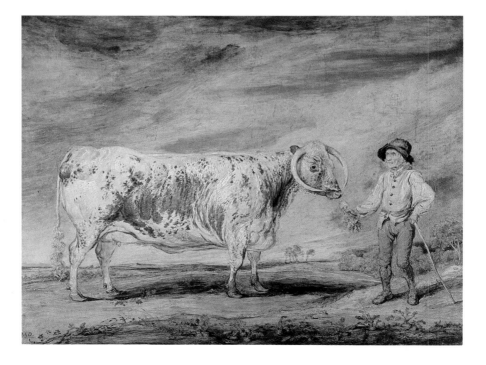

In 1867, when the 1st Duke of Abercorn was Viceroy of Ireland, there was a large houseparty at Viceregal Lodge, and amongst the guests there was the Lord Lieutenant of County Roscommon, Mr Edward King Tenison, and his wife Lady Louisa, daughter of the 1st Earl of Lichfield. Lady Louisa was, it seems, not very lovable; and the two youngest Abercorn sons, Lord Frederick and Lord Ernest, took the namecard from her bedroom door and placed it on the door of the only W.C. in the guest wing. So in those select ducal circles everyone began talking of going to Lady Louisa. Then as time went on, people became more familiar – Jimmy Abercorn told me that when he was a boy, one went to 'Lady Lou' (though he had never been told who Her Ladyship was).

Now, the courtesy title has been dropped, and within the last 30 years or so – only really since the war – the term has seeped down into general usage.

By 1880, the vast mortgage on the estate was beginning to be a source of worry. Following the agricultural depression of the 1870s, estate revenues had fallen dramatically, making the interest rates a serious drain on the property. Shugborough was saved by the energetic action of the 3rd Earl,

Thomas Francis. Born in 1856, he renewed the Anson/Coke connection by marrying at Holkham his first cousin twice removed, Lady Mildred Coke, daughter of the 2nd Earl of Leicester.

The 3rd Earl inherited Shugborough in 1892, but had already taken over the management of the estate in 1880 from his father, who did not feel up to facing a serious financial crisis at his age. His first action was to sack the agent, Robert Harvey Wyatt. Wyatt was the third generation of his family to have served as agent at Shugborough, having succeeded his father, Harvey Wyatt, and grandfather, also Robert Harvey Wyatt, appointed by Viscount Anson in the late eighteenth century. The last was the third son of William Wyatt, elder brother of the architects James and Samuel. Several different branches of the Wyatt family had served as hereditary land agents on estates throughout the nineteenth century, including Badminton, Croxteth, Culford, High Leigh and Penrhyn. By the late nineteenth century they were beginning to run out of steam and the burst of entrepreneurial brilliance which had pro-

Thomas, 3rd Earl of Lichfield (1856–1918) out shooting in 1906

duced over twenty architects and designers from the mid-eighteenth century onwards had reached its end. Robert Harvey Wyatt at Shugborough had, like his employer, been educated at Harrow and had a comfortable country house of his own. He was gentlemanly and reliable, but lacked the flexibility and drive needed to avert disaster.

The 3rd Earl (then still Viscount Anson) took over running the estate himself. His big task was to reduce the debts. He paid off the large mortgage with the Prudential Assurance Company and replaced it with several much smaller mortgages in the hands or friends or relations who were unlikely to foreclose. Like many late nineteenth-century landowners, he made up for the decline in agricultural rents from his estates by diversifying, investing money in the colonies, and taking on City directorships. He was, among other things, Deputy Governor of the Hudson's Bay Company, a director of the National Provident Bank of England and of the Bank of Australasia. Between 1880 and 1910, he put much of his own resources into the estate, as well as feeding all the estate income back for years, and he thus paid off large parts of the mortgage.[10] He tried to sell Ranton Abbey, but it failed to reach the asking price and so was let instead. Though sold later, it has been bought back by the present Lord Lichfield.

The 3rd Earl was devoted to Shugborough and fascinated by his family story. He made a lot of historical notes based on the archives, and re-arranged the contents of the house so as to emphasise their importance in relation to the family history. He rescued objects from outbuildings and brought them into the main house. 'Athenian' Stuart's carved doorcases and window shutters from the Temple of the Winds, for instance, were built into the Blue Drawing Room and Swallow Passage in the 1890s. Admiral Anson's fragile Chinese porcelain and Mirror Paintings, and even the chinoiserie plaster ceiling from the Chinese House, were carefully removed and transferred to the main house in 1885.

At the same time, the Georgian character of the rooms was restored, and new alterations were carefully made in the style of the original, using eighteenth-century chimney-pieces and other materials. The main part of this redecoration was carried out in 1899 by a well-known decorator, Amadée Joubert, who also worked at Lyme Park, Cheshire. It included alterations to the staircase, as well as embellishments to many of the principal rooms, though what became the billiard room was enlarged as late as 1911 to the design of the architect, H. L. Anderson.

The 3rd Earl also acquired several objects relating to Admiral Anson, including a portrait by Reynolds and a fragment of the lion figurehead from the *Centurion*. He was a keen naturalist and a good shot, spending much of his time out in the country watching wildlife. In the 1880s he formed at Shugborough a museum of stuffed birds, most of which is currently in store, though some can be seen in the County Museum in the stables and a few in the house. Like his father, he was public-spirited and devoted much effort to charitable work, being involved in many local societies, a supporter of the temperance movement and founder of the Social Welfare Association in London. He was killed in an accident while out shooting alone in 1918.

NOTES

1 Thomas Greville, *Memoirs*, III.

2 Ann Kettle, 'The Struggle for the Lichfield Interest', *Collections For a History of Staffordshire*, Fourth Series, VI (1970), pp.115–35.

3 John Martin Robinson, *The English Country Estate* (1988), pp.121–7.

4 C. Hussey, op. cit.

5 I am most grateful to Miss Pamela Sambrook who kindly made available to me information about the 1st Earl of Lichfield's financial position, arising from her research into the finances of the Shugborough estate as a whole in the nineteenth century, derived from the family archives and their bank account at Coutts.

6 C. Hussey, op. cit.

7 *Notes from the Life of an Ordinary Mortal* (1911), p.114.

8 *Survey of London*, op. cit., p.153.

9 Morant & Boyd's bills are preserved in the Anson papers in the Staffordshire Record Office. They would repay detailed study by a Victorian furniture historian.

10 Ex. info Miss Pamela Sambrook.

CHAPTER FIVE

THE TWENTIETH CENTURY

On the death of the 3rd Earl in 1918, he was succeeded by his son, Thomas Edward, who married first Evelyn, daughter of Colonel Edward George Keppel, and secondly Margaret, daughter of Colonel Henry Dawson-Greene. Thomas Edward was born in 1883. He was ADC and Acting Master of the Horse to the Lord Lieutenant of Ireland from 1906 to 1910, and served in the Great War as a captain in the London Rifle Brigade. After succeeding to the title, he devoted himself to the care of Shugborough.

Thanks to his father's timely and successful reduction of the nineteenth-century mortgages on the estate, the 4th Earl did not face the serious financial problems which beset traditional landowners in the early 1920s and which led to the sale and eventual demolition of several other Staffordshire houses. The main crisis to face Shugborough in these years was a very severe outbreak of dry rot caused by water seeping through Samuel Wyatt's patent slate facing of the exterior and then spreading through the structure behind. In 1920 the whole of

Thomas, 4th Earl of Lichfield (1883–1960), by Frank Eastman (Staircase Hall), (detail)

Patrick, 5th Earl of Lichfield (b.1939), by Nigel Waymouth

the exterior of the house was stripped, and the slate replaced by stucco. At the same time the central bay on the west front was remodelled, the windows lengthened, pilasters added and the three original attic windows replaced with a high parapet containing a central *oeil-de-boeuf* window. This was done under the direction of the architect Alan Munby.

During the Second World War the estate, which is intersected by two main line railways, was of considerable strategic significance and a large military camp was constructed over most of the southern part of the park. Some damage was done to the park buildings, especially the Tower of the Winds, and traces of the military hutments lingered on for years after the war.

Lord and Lady Lichfield did their best to restore Shugborough after the War and it was their wish that the property should be preserved and opened to the public. Consequently, on the 4th Earl's death in 1960 the house, park and contents were offered in part payment of death duties to the National Trust, to which the family trustees also gave a sum of money to provide an endowment fund. The income from this fund is not sufficient to provide for the heavy cost of upkeep, and in a far-seeing manner Staffordshire County Council agreed to accept a lease of Shugborough. It was largely due to Margaret, Lady Lichfield, that these complicated negotiations were carried through to a successful conclusion. Under the resulting arrangements, the County Council has established a County Museum in the stables, and uses part of the estate for education and recreation purposes, as well as administering the property. The County Council with the assistance of the National Trust has since carried out extensive restoration both of the house and the park buildings.

The 4th Earl was succeeded in the earldom by his grandson, who has established a reputation as one of the leading professional photographers of the day, under the name of Patrick Lichfield. With his three children, he continues to live in the private part of the house.

CHAPTER SIX
THE HOUSE

THE HALL

The door from Samuel Wyatt's portico leads straight into the entrance hall, which he remodelled as an interesting geometrical space in 1794 for the 1st Viscount Anson. Part of the original seventeenth-century house, its oval shape was produced by Wyatt's introduction of eight Siena marble scagliola columns supplied by Joseph Alcott. The Doric capitals, based on those found at the Temple of Apollo at Delos, have a fluted band round the top, and are among the earliest uses of this order in English architecture. The plaster-work frieze, by Joseph Rose the Younger, incorporates the Anson crest, a spearhead issuing from a ducal coronet, in the metopes, the usual way of displaying heraldry in the entrance halls of eighteenth-century houses. The Pompeian red of the walls copies the original colour and has recently been restored. Cream paint was cleaned off the scagliola columns by John Fowler as part of his redecoration of the house *c.*1968.

This austere, but noble, Classical *vestibulum* was intended by Wyatt as a setting for the finest Greek and Roman sculpture collected by Thomas Anson. The majority of the sarcophagi and statues were sold in 1842, but some pieces still remain and are displayed in this room.

The Hall

SCULPTURE

A large pair of plaster casts of centaurs stand in the two alcoves. Taken by Bartolomeo Cavaceppi from the original Greek sculptures in the Capitoline Museum in Rome, these were bought by Thomas Anson in 1765 through the agency of Joseph Nollekens. They stood originally in the ground floor of the Tower of the Winds. The pair of antique Roman marble tablets beyond them are carved in bas-relief, one with the figure of a poet, the other with *Pomona holding a basket of fruit* (the head a later addition). The marble figure to the left of the Saloon door also represents Pomona, while the group on the right is of Castor and Pollux – both thought to be eighteenth-century copies after the antique.

THE BUST PARLOUR

The name of this small room derives from Thomas Anson's celebrated collection of antique sculpture, for some of his Greek and Roman busts were displayed here before their dispersal in 1842. The chimney-piece, brought from elsewhere in the house and only set up here in 1899, is a fine piece of Rococo woodcarving, close in spirit to some of the designs of Matthias Lock. The striped wallpaper was made by Coles and chosen for the room around 1968 by John Fowler.

SCULPTURE

The white marble group of Cupid and Psyche is French, late eighteenth century.

PICTURES

1 *Venus Directing Cupids to Chastise Pan*
Manner of Filippo Lauri (1623–94)
This is a variant of a much repeated composition by Lauri, in which Venus orders Pan to be transfixed with the dart of love.

2 *The Ruins*
Nicholas Dall, ARA (fl.1756–d.1776)
Signed and dated 1775
These are situated opposite the west front of the house, on the river bank, and incorporate fragments of earlier buildings at Shugborough. For a preparatory drawing see No. 71.

3 *Oakedge*
Nicholas Dall, ARA (fl.1756–d.1776)
Signed and dated 1775
Situated near Weetmans Bridge on the south side of the Stafford–Rugeley road, Oakedge was bought by Thomas Anson in 1768. It was demolished in the

latter half of the nineteenth century. For a preparatory drawing, see No. 61.

48 *The East Front of Shugborough*
Moses Griffith (1747–1819)
Pen and wash
Done for the engraving in Thomas Pennant's *Journey from Chester to London* (1782).

The two canvases by Nicolas Dall serve as a prelude to the unrivalled series of topographical views of Shugborough Park and its surroundings which are displayed in different rooms of the house.

FURNITURE AND CERAMICS

The giltwood mirror above the chimney-piece is Venetian, mid-eighteenth-century, and a pair with one in the State Bedroom. The two large celadon vases on the mantelpiece are of Chinese porcelain with Louis XVI ormolu mounts.

THE ANTE ROOM

This little room formed the linking section between the main block and Wright's northern pavilion, built between 1745 and 1748. It was originally lit by a round-headed window, and the recess opposite was devised for a large-scale model of Admiral Anson's famous ship, the *Centurion*, in which he circumnavigated the world.

The double doors to the Blue Drawing Room were inserted by Samuel Wyatt in 1794 and he was also responsible for the present arrangement of the four niches, the thin pilaster panels round the walls and the tripartite sash window of a type known at the time as a 'Wyatt Window'. The original glazing bars here and elsewhere in the house are of metal, not of wood, to ensure the slimmest possible section. In the nineteenth century this room was used as the servery to the Dining Room, and the polished steel hotplate cupboard dates from the installation of central heating at the turn of the century.

SCULPTURE

Before the sale in 1842 six of the finest of Thomas Anson's marble statues stood in this room. Now, in the two outer niches are marble busts of Admiral Lord Anson (1697–1762) and his wife, Lady Elizabeth Yorke, daughter of the 1st Earl of Hardwicke, attributed to Joseph Wilton. The busts of Homer and Seneca in the inner niches are copies after antique originals from the Farnese collection, now in the Naples Museum.

PICTURES

4 (?) *Thomas Anson* (1695–1773)
Manner of John Vanderbank (*c.*1694–1739)
This was bought by the 3rd Earl in 1895 as a portrait of Admiral Anson. This seems unlikely, but it may represent his brother, Thomas Anson.

5 *1st Earl of Lichfield* (1795–1854)
(?) Thomas Phillips, RA (1770–1845)
Monogrammed and dated 1819, but possibly a copy of the engraving
He is seen in the Library at Shugborough.

FURNITURE AND CERAMICS

The pair of Chinese painted mirror pictures flanking the window, two of the finest of their kind in existence, originally hung in the Chinese House, erected in the garden in 1747. Their oriental hardwood and parcel-gilt frames are designed in a European idiom. This would agree with contemporary accounts that Admiral Anson acquired most of the furniture for

One of the Chinese painted mirror pictures in the Ante Room brought back from China by Admiral Anson

the building when in China earlier in the same decade. A pair of *famille verte* tureens with covers, of the K'ang Hsi period, are reputed to be part of the Admiral's everyday service (dating from 1720 or slightly later), most of which is in the Blue Drawing Room.

The cartonnier on an ebonised dwarf cabinet, one of the French pieces acquired by the 2nd Earl of Lichfield in the 1850s, bears the stamp of the *ébéniste*, Philippe-Claude Montigny (*maître* in 1766).

THE DINING ROOM

Of essentially Palladian proportions, 38ft × 24ft, this large room forms part of Thomas Anson's additions to the house, completed about 1748, and was almost certainly designed by Thomas Wright of Durham. Until 1794 it served as the drawing-room, and there were originally doors on the west wall leading to a bedchamber and dressing-room behind.

The elaborate Rococo plasterwork of the frieze, the coved ceiling, overmantel and picture frames, were executed by an Italian stuccadore named Vassalli, either Francesco or Giovanni, both of whom were recorded in England at this date.

The central panel is after Guido Reni's celebrated painting of *Apollo and the Hours preceded by Aurora* in the casino of the Palazzo Rospigliosi in Rome. The medallion heads in the cove are unusual in that they represent the Egyptian deities, Isis and Serapis, together with the Greek Dionysus and his attendant Maenad: a strange choice which again suggests that Thomas Wright, with his interest in astronomy and the occult, was responsible for the general decorative scheme.

The splendid marble chimney-piece, with Bacchic mask and garlands of vines, was probably installed here when this first became a dining-room during Samuel Wyatt's alterations of 1794. On the other hand, the style of the chimney-piece is consistent with that of Thomas Wright's work of the 1740s, so may originally have been made for the previous dining-room. The sculptor is not known but could be Peter Scheemakers, who did other work for Thomas Anson. The present colour scheme of different shades of grey and pale blue with touches of white and gold was devised by John Fowler in the late 1960s.

PICTURES

Eight architectural capriccios

Nicholas Dall (fl.1756–d.1776) and (?) Others

The exact history of these pictures is hard to determine, because they have been cut up and spliced to

The Dining Room, with architectural paintings by Nicholas Dall, portrait of Admiral Anson by William Hoare, chimney-piece attributed to Peter Scheemakers and plasterwork by Vassalli

accommodate them to the alterations of the room, and their mixed techniques, combined with unhappy attempts at restoration, have greatly altered their appearance.

The first that we hear of them is in 1748, when Philip Yorke recorded in his travel journal that the room had been 'ornamented in Stucco, and with large Pictures of Architecture painted at Bologna'. The better-preserved parts of the large oblong oil painting on the far wall bear this out: they could well be by a Bolognese specialist in scenographic paintings, such as Pietro Paltronieri, known as Il Mirandolese dalle Prospettive.

Twenty-two years later, Nicholas Dall, who seems originally to have been invited to Shugborough to paint views of the house and its grounds (Nos. 2, 16, 33, 45, 56 and 68) produced designs for decorative pictures on one wall of the Library (unspecified) and for the Orangery an oil painting of the Temple of Minerva Polias. It would appear that he was at the same time asked to renew the paintings in this room. They may well have suffered or have been weakened during their long voyage to England, for William Gilpin talks of the room being 'hung with large Ruins in distemper by Dahl' in 1772.

In 1794 the room was made into a dining-room, the doors to the former bedchamber and dressing-room were sealed up, and the frames and paintings on either side of them enlarged to occupy the vacant space. The painting on the end wall of the Library was probably taken down and cut into two to fit, since the signs of splicing in these two compositions are only too apparent. Biagio Rebecca, who was paid for un-specified painting at that time, may also have been involved, as something was probably also done to disguise the discrepancy between those parts of the decoration that were executed in oils, and those that were carried out in distemper, resulting in friable strata of overpaint. Successive restorations have only compounded the problem, and the National Trust is currently trying to discover whether enough original paint remains to make restoration worthwhile.

5a *Admiral Lord Anson* (1697–1762)
William Hoare, RA (1707–92)
George Anson, circumnavigator and admiral. After his victory over the French at Cape Finisterre in 1747, he was made a Baron, and this portrait of him in his peer's robes was probably painted to celebrate the fact.

FURNITURE

The pair of white and gilt pier tables, their aprons carved with masks of Hercules and lion pelts, are let into the skirting board, and are probably part of the original furniture of the room, having been bought in at the 1842 sale. They are very close to a design by Matthias Lock in the Victoria and Albert Museum. The pair of white marble urns which they support are late eighteenth century.

The very large semi-circular mahogany sideboard with ormolu mounts, fitted into the bay window, dates from 1794, when this first became the dining-room. It was almost certainly designed by Samuel Wyatt and is an unusual piece for, unlike his brother James or Robert Adam, he rarely designed the fur-niture for his neo-Classical interiors himself. The four tall sheets of mirror plate between the windows probably date from the early 1830s. The contem-porary curtains of red satin and green velvet, with gold braid and fringe, and with the Anson arms and Earl's coronet in ormolu fixed in the centre, are no longer hung because of their fragile condition, but the pelmets are still in place.

The late eighteenth-century dining-room table is on loan from Osterley Park, London, and the grained sideboards at either end of the room are from Attingham Park, Shropshire. The Louis XVI ormolu mantel clock has a movement by Roggen, and is

Silver punchbowl with engraving of HMS *Centurion*, 1768 (Dining Room)

flanked by two Derbyshire blue-john vases with ormolu mounts by Matthew Boulton. The good nineteenth-century English carpet was supplied by Brookfield Successors Ltd of Stafford.

SILVER-GILT, SILVER AND GLASS

The family silver was not included in the 1842 sale with the result that some fine examples survive in the house: the large silver candelabrum in the centre of the dining-room table is by Robert Garrard, dated 1855; the four Corinthian column candlesticks by Emick Romer, 1762; and the pair with stems in the form of amorini by Ernest Sieber, 1747. Also on the table are a silver statuette of St Michael overcoming the devil, engraved on the plinth *John Flaxman E.F. Rome 1785* (it is a copy of the original marble at Petworth, Sussex), three silver vase-shaped casters made by Anne Craig and John Neville about 1750, and a set of rare Hanover funnel-shaped glasses with gilt rims dating from about 1740. There is a similar set at Buckingham Palace.

On the sideboards at either end of the room are a pair of circular silver salvers engraved with the arms of Admiral Lord Anson, by Paul de Lamerie, 1747; and a pair of silver two-handled cups and covers, presented to Viscount Anson, later 4th Earl of Lichfield, on his coming of age in 1904.

On the semi-circular sideboard in the bay window is a silver punchbowl with engravings of HMS *Centurion* and the arms of Admiral Lord Anson (Argent three bends engrailed gules with a crescent gules in the cantel), by Daniel Smith and Robert Sharp, 1768; a silver-gilt ewer by Paul Storr, 1800; a silver-gilt vase and cover by Bernard & Co. presented as a trophy at the Leamington Spring Races in 1829; and another given as a christening present to the Hon. William Anson by the Duchess of Kent in 1834.

The Blue Drawing Room

THE BLUE DRAWING ROOM

The segmental apse at the west end of the room and the characteristic tripartite window, together with the simple Classical cornice and skirting, were designed by Samuel Wyatt. The carved wooden window-shutters and doorcases are, however, from 'Athenian' Stuart's Temple of the Winds in the park, along with the frames to the two mirrors on the inside wall, which were originally window-surrounds. They were moved here as part of Amadée Joubert's alterations in 1899. The marble chimney-piece is by John Deval the Younger (1793) and the gilt fillet round the walls and in the corners of the room was supplied by the famous wallpaper makers, Eckhardt & Co., in May 1795.

FURNITURE AND CERAMICS

The room contains a number of eighteenth-century pieces, either Chinese or English in the Chinese taste. The large mahogany display cabinet, which is close to a design in Chippendale's *Director* (1754), contains porcelain largely brought back from China by Admiral Anson, including some *famille verte* dishes (*c.*1725) from the same service as the tureens in the Ante Room. The very rare Yung Ch'eng *famille rose* 'eggshell' lanterns (jars of translucent porcelain in which lights were placed) came originally from the Chinese House in the garden. They too were brought back from China in 1744 by the Admiral. The three large early eighteenth-century Imari vases on their original oriental stands painted red and gold also came from the Chinese House. The pair of Ch'ien Lung *famille rose* rectangular ink stands are also fine examples of Chinese porcelain of similar date.

The pair of exceptionally beautiful carved and gilded mirror frames, one of which retains its original Chinese mirror painting, is the work of one of the leading London carvers of the day, quite possibly Chippendale himself. The two Japanese black lacquer cabinets on English gilt stands date from about 1710, while the late eighteenth-century Chinese cloisonné enamel and gilt pieces including a set of jardinières at the other end of the room are said to have come from the Summer Palace in Peking in 1860.

There are two pieces of French furniture, acquired by the 2nd Earl of Lichfield: a fine Louis XIV giltwood barometer (with an inscription recording that it was 'réparé en 1842'), and a tulipwood bow-fronted commode of the Régence period. Near the window is an early nineteenth-century loo table in the style of Gillows, with a mahogany base and laburnum, or *lignum vitae*, top.

PICTURES

To the right of the window hangs a Classical landscape by Zuccarelli in an outstanding carved and gilt Rococo frame, gently curved to follow the line of the wall. Its companion was unfortunately sold in 1842, but a copy (with a new frame) was provided by Morant & Boyd for the 2nd Earl in 1855.

6 *A Landscape with Figures*
Unknown, nineteenth-century
Painted to form a pair to No. 7.

7 *A classical Landscape with Peasants fording a Stream*
Francesco Zuccarelli, RA (1702–88)
Probably acquired from the artist during his stay in England in 1752–62 or 1765–71. Bought back in the sale of 1842.

THE RED DRAWING ROOM

The largest and most impressive interior at Shugborough, this room was created in 1794 by Samuel Wyatt. The segmental ceiling is decorated with beautiful plasterwork by Joseph Rose the Younger; its neo-Classical ornament, with anthemions, lyres, delicate wreaths and sprays of acanthus, is characteristic of Wyatt's last work. The long rectangular bas-reliefs of figures at either end, 'suspended' by chains from a central rosette, are particularly successful.

The elegant chimney-piece of white marble with ormolu mounts was supplied by Richard Westmacott the Younger. The walls were originally covered by Eckhardt & Co. with 'varnished Silver linen on a Salmon ground'. This had long since disappeared when, in 1965, the present striped wallpaper was introduced by John Fowler, reusing Eckhardt's original moulded gilt borders.

FURNITURE

The vast overmantel mirror and pier glasses were made for this room in 1794, and were a great technical achievement at the time. The English cut-glass chandelier is of the same decade and may also be original to the room, like the set of '14 large square arm'd chairs', with '2 large sophas to match . . . the frames richly carved and gilt, on castors', which were again supplied in 1794, by the London upholsterers Charles Smith & Co. Their bill, for a total of £296, included 'Shamey Leather stockings' to protect the legs of the chairs from being knocked by over-zealous housemaids. Designed in a thoroughgoing French style, this seat furniture would originally have been placed round the

The Red Drawing Room

walls and the backs of the frames are not therefore decorated.

The pair of white and gold pier tables with rare green *cippolino* marble tops, and two gilt tripod stands decorated with rams' masks, are earlier in date and thought to be among the few surviving contributions made by 'Athenian' Stuart to the interior of the house in the 1760s. Their marble tops were acquired at Rome, from Scarpellino's in the Campo Vaccino, by Joseph Nollekens on behalf of Thomas Anson and cost 85 *scudi*.*

The *pietra dura* top to the gilt table, with a central oval panel showing two lions in a fanciful landscape, is Florentine, and was probably acquired by Thomas

* there were four Roman *scudi* to the English pound.

Anson in Italy. The top dates from the early seventeenth century, but the base is mid-nineteenth.

The remainder of the furniture is mostly French, and was acquired by the 2nd Earl of Lichfield in the mid-nineteenth century. It is well suited to the Francophile elegance of Samuel Wyatt's decoration and includes (starting from the window side of the door and continuing clockwise): a Louis XVI mahogany upright *secrétaire* bearing the stamp of J. H. Riesener, one of the most celebrated of all Parisian *ébénistes*; a Louis XV marquetry bureau; a Régence kingwood commode of *bombé* form; a Louis XVI upright *secrétaire*; a kingwood commode with fine ormolu mounts, by Louis Delaître *c*.1740; a breakfront commode in the so-called 'transitional style' of about 1765, the front and sides with vases of flowers in shaped marquetry panels; another fine Louis XV marquetry commode signed by Joseph Schmidt (*maître* in 1761); and finally, to the left of the door, a Louis XV mahogany upright *secrétaire* inlaid with satinwood and kingwood, by the Westphalian-born François Rubestuck. The large *fleur de pêche* marble vase with ormolu mounts in front of the central window is of the Louis XVI period.

The Aubusson carpet is on loan from the Fairhaven Collection, Anglesey Abbey, Cambridgeshire.

CERAMICS

On the mantelpiece are a pair of Meissen candelabra, modelled by J. J. Kändler, and a Louis XV ormolu clock with a movement by Moisy of Paris, and incorporating Meissen porcelain figures and Vincennes flowers. Other pieces displayed on the tables and cabinets round the sides of the room include a large Louis XVI ormolu clock with the striking movement by Julien le Roy and the case formed as an urn with satyrs' masks, flanked by cupids emblemmatic of Sculpture and Geography, a pair of Minton urn-shaped vases in the Sèvres style, which complements the pairs of genuine Sèvres vases with ormolu mounts, in *bleu-du-roi*, bought by the 2nd Earl of Lichfield.

PICTURES

A few remnants of Thomas Anson's once famous collection of pictures survive here, including a variant of Honthorst's *The Angel appearing to St Peter*, once thought to be by Guido Reni, and a version of Guido's *Susannah and the Elders*, as well as the Meléndez *Immaculate Conception*. The two 'Guidos' were acquired by Thomas Anson as a pair and were bought back at the 1842 sale for £262 10s each.

8 *Louisa, Countess of Lichfield with two of her Children*
(d. 1879)
Sir George Hayter (1792–1871)
Signed and dated 1832
Louisa, daughter of Nathaniel Philips, married Thomas Lord Anson, later 1st Earl of Lichfield, in 1819. Her eldest son, Thomas, later 2nd Earl, and her daughter Harriet, who married the 6th Lord Vernon, are seen with her.

9 *The Angel appearing to St Peter*
After Gerard Honthorst (1590–1656)
The figure of St Peter is a copy or version of *The Liberation of St Peter* in East Berlin. The angel is a later interpolation in the style of Guido Reni, added before the painting was bought – as an exceptional Reni – by Thomas Anson from Sir John Dick, Consul at Leghorn, in 1765.

10 *The Immaculate Conception*
Miguel Jacinto Meléndez (1679–1736)
Signed and dated 1731
Inspired by Murillo. The signature records the artist's position as painter to the King, Philip V. He was the elder brother of the portrait-painter Francisco Antonio, and uncle of the still-life painter, Luis.

11 *Susannah and the Elders*
After Guido Reni (1575–1642)
Other versions of the composition exist. The prime one is in the National Gallery, London.

12 *Lord Anson's Hunt*
William Webb (1780–1846)
Hounds and hunt servants on Cannock Chase. Lord Anson's grey horse is awaiting him. See the companion picture, No. 13.

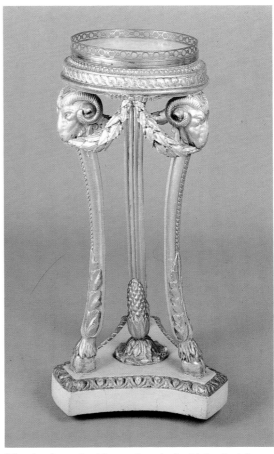

Gilt tripod stand with rams' masks by 'Athenian' Stuart (Red Drawing Room)

13 *Lord Anson's Hunt*
William Webb (1780–1846)
Painted in 1827
Lord Anson (later 1st Earl of Lichfield) is mounted in the centre. Among others represented are Lord Howe on a grey horse at the left, with Lord Alvanley next to him, Mr Norbury riding a grey at the right, William Coke dismounted at the extreme right, and George Anson (later General Sir George Anson) between them. The scene is near Atherstone, with Bardon Hill on the horizon and Mancetter and Witherley churches visible in the middle distance. The pack, in existence by 1820, continued to be known as Lord Anson's Hunt until 1830, when on his appointment as Master of the Royal Buckhounds it became, as it has since remained, the Atherstone Hunt.
Pair to No. 12.

14 *Thomas Anson, later 1st Earl of Lichfield; Anna, later Countess of Rosebery; and George Anson, as Children*
Anne Margaret, Viscountess Anson (1778–1843)
Signed and dated
The three eldest children of the 1st Viscount Anson, painted in 1799 by their mother, an accomplished artist.

15 *An Allegorical Portrait Group commemorating the Victory at Quiberon Bay in 1759*
English, *c.*1759
George II seated at the left is shown the Fleet by William Pitt the Elder. The victorious Admiral Hawke stands at the right with Lord Anson, then First Lord of the Admiralty. In the sky above, a winged figure is about to crown the king with a wreath; Britannia looks down upon Pitt; Fame hovers over the two admirals.

THE SWALLOW PASSAGE

So-called because of the habitual nesting of swallows outside in the angle of Samuel Wyatt's verandah, this has another, simple Classical frieze of the 1790s, and gilt borders supplied by Eckhardt. The shutters were again brought from the Temple of the Winds by Joubert in 1899 as part of the 3rd Earl's alterations to the house.

FURNITURE AND CERAMICS
The black lacquer longcase clock, with a movement by Andrew Padbery of Bishop's Waltham, has in the arch of the dial a representation of the *Prince George*, Admiral Anson's flagship at the battle off Cape Finisterre, and the date of the battle, 3 May 1747. A pair of somewhat comic dolphins and a trident are carved in the cresting above. The two bronze vases are probably seventeeth-century Italian 'after the antique' and the large Wedgwood pottery urn in mottled colours, or Agateware, intended to resemble porphyry, is close in form to Louis XVI marble prototypes. The handles in the form of rams' heads and the oval medallions of Cupid and Psyche are gilded in emulation of ormolu mounts.

PICTURES
16 *A View of Shugborough and the Park from the East*
Nicholas Dall, ARA (fl.1756–d.1776)
Nicholas Dall's large view of Shugborough and the park from the east, probably painted about 1768, shows the house as altered by Thomas Wright, and before the heightening of the links between the main block and pavilions. On the other hand it shows most of Stuart's monuments already complete: the Triumphal Arch, Temple of the Winds and Lanthorn of Demosthenes on the left, with the earlier Chinese Pagoda (no longer surviving) and the roofs of what was left of the old village of Shugborough, where Park Farm is now. In the background at the left, the neigbouring estate of Tixall; at the right Ingestre.

STAIRCASE HALL AND LANDING

Though probably occupying the site of the staircase in the original 1693 house, this has been much altered – by Wyatt in 1794, by Joubert in 1899, and finally in about 1920. Wyatt's plasterwork anthemion frieze still remains as do his metal balustrades of characteristic design, with cast and gilt honeysuckle ornaments supplied by the firm of Underwood & Co. The mahogany stair-rail is inlaid with satinwood and ebony stringing. Joubert was responsible for the present moulded ceiling (which probably replaced a skylight) and for opening the arches on the west side so as to give a new source of light. But the 'Venetian window' opening on to the north landing was only made between the First and Second World Wars in place of a Victorian stained-glass window.

The tapestry, representing *Earth* (from a set of the *Elements*) with Ceres and Proserpine, was probably woven by John Vanderbank at the Soho Manufactory in London in the early eighteenth century. It is closely based on a panel of the Gobelins *Elements*, designed by Le Brun a generation earlier.

The Staircase Hall, with
Wyatt's honeysuckle
pattern metal balustrade

Soho tapestry of *Earth* (from a set of the *Elements*), probably by John Vanderbank (Staircase Hall)

FURNITURE AND SCULPTURE

At the foot of the stairs, the massive bronze bust of Demosthenes set in marble drapery is an early nineteenth-century copy after the antique. The tripod or *Athénienne* is attributed to 'Athenian' Stuart. The sedan chair in the neo-Classical taste belonged to Anne Margaret, Viscountess Anson, after 1806 and bears her monogram and coronet, while the rest of the furniture includes a harewood *bonheur-du-jour* with a Sèvres plaque in the Louis XVI style (in store), and a display cabinet containing mostly Meissen and Crown Derby porcelain. A glazed alcove on the first-floor landing contains some very good late eighteenth-century Stourbridge, Irish and other glass, including a pair of finely cut ice-pails with pineapple finials and silver-gilt mounts dated 1802, a pair of fluted water jugs with silver-gilt mounts dated 1798, two Victorian Claret jugs also with silver-gilt mounts and a pair of moulded and fluted English jugs of the late seventeenth century, possibly Ravenscroft.

PICTURES

The paintings include several family portraits and one or two further remnants of Thomas Anson's collection of Old Masters.

17 *Apollo as Shepherd*
Italian, seventeenth-century
Circular, bought in at the 1842 sale, when attributed to Rosa da Tivoli.

18 *Architectural Ruins*
(?) Angelo Maria Costa (fl. early eighteenth-century)
Possibly this is by Costa's pupil, Coccorante.

19 *Romulus and Remus with the Tiber River God*
Roman, eighteenth-century
Apparently an allegory of Rome as they were the legendary founders of the city.

20 *Still Life with dead Game*
After (?) Candido Vitali (1680–1753)

21 *A Landscape with a Herdsman*
Dutch (?) seventeenth-century

22 *Cows and Sheep in a Landscape*
Karel Desan (fl.1829–48)
Panel signed and dated 1848

23 *Admiral Boscawen* (1711–61)
After Allan Ramsay (1713–84)
Boscawen fought under Anson at Cape Finisterre, and was Admiral of the Blue during Anson's second term of office as 1st Lord.

24 *Anna Margaret Anson, Countess of Rosebery* (d.1882)
Thomas Barber (c.1768–1843)
Eldest daughter of Viscount Anson and second wife of the 4th Earl of Rosebery, whom she married in 1819.

25 *1st Earl of Lichfield* (1795–1854)
Chester Harding (1792–1866)
Dated 1824 on the back of the canvas. Harding, an American portrait painter, first visited England in 1823.

26 *Animals sheltering in a Storm*
After Philip de Loutherbourg, RA (1740–1812)

27 *Admiral Lord Anson* (1697–1762)
Arthur Pond (1701–58)
As a young man; engraved by Grignion in 1744.

28 *General Sir William Anson, 1st Bt* (1772–1847)
Thomas Barber (c.1768–1843)
Fifth son of George Anson and Mary Vernon; created a baronet in 1831.

29 *General Sir George Anson* (1769–1849)
Thomas Barber (c.1768–1843)
Inscribed on stretcher and dated 1815
Second son of George Anson and Mary Vernon; Governor of Chelsea Hospital.

30 *A Naval Officer*
English, mid-eighteenth-century
Formerly said to be Lord Anson, it may represent one of his officers who accompanied him on his voyage of circumnavigation. However, it is more likely to be Lord Anson's nephew, Thomas Adams, who entered the navy and was killed at the Battle of Pondicherry in 1748.

31 *Colonel the Hon. Augustus Anson, VC* (1835–1900)
English, late nineteenth-century
Third son of the 1st Earl of Lichfield. Painted from a photograph.

32 *3rd Earl of Lichfield* (1856–1918)
Frank Moss Bennett (1874–1953)
Signed and dated 1920
Painted from a photograph.

33 *An extensive View of the Park and Monuments*
Nicholas Dall, ARA (fl.1756–d.1776)
Signed and dated 1768
In the centre, the Triumphal Arch; at the right the Pagoda and Lanthorn of Demosthenes; at the left the Cascade and Tower of the Winds. For a preparatory drawing, see No. 56.

34 *Three Children of the 1st Earl of Lichfield*
A. E. Chalon, RA (1780–1860)
Watercolour, signed and dated 1838
The eldest boy is Thomas, later 2nd Earl, the others
are not certainly identifiable.

35 *William Anson of Shugborough* (1656–1720)
English, late seventeenth-century
Father of the Admiral and of Thomas Anson.

36 *4th Earl of Lichfield* (1883–1960)
Frank Eastman
Signed and dated 1936
Painted from a photograph.

37 *Anne Margaret Coke, Viscountess Anson*
(1778–1843)
Thomas Barber (c.1768–1843)
Daughter of Thomas Coke, afterwards 1st Earl of
Leicester, and wife of the 1st Viscount Anson, whom
she married in 1794.

THE BIRD ROOM
(OPEN OCCASIONALLY)

This is now the drawing-room of Lord Lichfield's
private quarters and is the work of Samuel Wyatt. It
has a characteristic ceiling of etiolated Wyatt pattern
with plasterwork by Joseph Rose the Younger incorporating motifs from the Anson arms, and a screen of
marbled columns along one side. The present decoration was evolved by David Mlinaric in the 1960s, one
of his earliest works. This room is so called because
it was used by the 3rd Earl of Lichfield, a keen
naturalist and ornithologist, to display his large
collection of stuffed birds (which are now mainly in
store). Originally this room would have served the
purpose of an upstairs saloon from which access was
gained to the different parts of the house. The
chimney-piece of white and Siena marble is the finest
to survive from the first, more Rococo, phase of
Thomas Anson's remodelling of Shugborough.

The Bird Room

PICTURES

The landscape facing the fireplace is by William Barker of Bath. The pair of Boulle cabinets on ebonised stands bought by the 2nd Earl are typical of the luxury French furniture acquired by English antiquarian collectors in the early nineteenth century.

THE STATE BEDROOM AND SITTING ROOM

The steps leading up from the corridor at the top of the stairs have bannisters taken from Stuart's Temple of the Winds and installed here by Joubert in 1899. Samuel Wyatt's principal guest apartment consisted of three rooms with chaste neo-Classical cornices and chimney-pieces, and once again with gilt borders by Eckhardt & Co. supplied in 1794. (The former dressing-room is now a bedroom and not on view.)

FURNITURE

The original state bed and all the accompanying furniture by Charles Smith & Co. were sold in 1842 and, apart from a Boulle bureau with an inlaid top in the style of Berain, the two rooms are now furnished with solid Victorian pieces acquired by the 2nd Earl of Lichfield during the 1850s, when he bought the house back to life. The bed itself is upholstered in crimson damask, and the braided valances match the curtains (now in store). The Brussels weave carpet in both rooms was recently remade in Bradford to the original 1850s pattern (seen lining the mahogany bedsteps). The gilt mirror above the dressing-table is Venetian, and the overmantel glass in the bedchamber is nineteenth-century in the Chinese Chippendale style. The set of china on the washstand is Copeland.

PICTURES

In 1855 the 2nd Earl of Lichfield married Lady Harriet Hamilton, one of the fourteen children of the 1st Duke of Abercorn, and pastel portraits of herself and five of her brothers and sisters by Jules Massé hang here, together with studies of animals by Sir Edwin Landseer, who was a close friend of her parents.

STATE SITTING ROOM

91 *Evelyn, Countess of Lichfield, with her Children*
Charlotte Blakeney Ward (fl. early twentieth century)
Pastel, signed
She was the daughter of Colonel Edward Keppel and wife of the 4th Earl of Lichfield.

92–97 *Portraits of six of the fourteen Children of the 1st Duke of Abercorn*
Jules Massé (1825–99)
All pastel, signed
Apparently painted in the early 1850s.

92 *Lady Louisa Hamilton* (d.1912)
Wife of the 6th Duke of Buccleuch.

93 *Viscount Hamilton* (1838–1913)
Eldest son; succeeded his father as 2nd Duke in 1885.

94 *Lady Beatrice Hamilton* (d.1871)
Wife of the 2nd Earl of Durham.

95 *Lady Harriet Hamilton* (d.1913)
Wife of the 2nd Earl of Lichfield.

96 *Lord Claud Hamilton* (1843–1925)
Second son.

97 *Lady Katherine Hamilton* (d.1874)
Wife of the 4th Earl of Mount Edgcumbe.

98 *Two Daughters of the 1st Earl of Lichfield*
(?) Anne Coke, Lady Anson (1778–1843)
Watercolour

ON ROUND TABLE

51 *Anne, Countess of Leicester, and her Daughter*
William Derby (1786–1847)
Pencil and watercolour, signed and dated 1832
Lady Anne Keppel, second wife of the 1st Earl of Leicester whom she married in 1822; her daughter Margaret married Sir Archibald Macdonald, 3rd Bt, in 1849.

52 *Lady Harriet Hamilton, Countess of Lichfield* (d.1913)
English, nineteenth-century
Watercolour

99 *1st Earl of Lichfield* (1795–1854)
Karl Goebel (1824–79)
Watercolour, signed and dated 1849
He suffered severely from gout and went often for the cure to Gräffenburg, where this drawing was made.

100 *Viscount Hamilton and Lady Harriet Hamilton with a Fortune-Teller*
Sir Edwin Landseer, RA (1802–73)
Pencil, signed and dated 1843

101 *'Frank looking pleasant'*
Sir John Leslie (1822–1916)
Pen and pencil
A sketch of the 10th Earl of Wemyss who married Lady Anne Anson, eldest daughter of the 1st Earl of Lichfield, in 1843.

102–5 These drawings by Sir Edwin Landseer, RA (1802–73) were probably brought to Shugborough by Harriet, wife of the 2nd Earl of Lichfield.

102 *Six Studies of Animals*
Pencil on one mount, dated 1844

103 *Seven Studies*
Pencil on one mount

104 *A Cat watching a Mousehole*
Pencil, signed

105 *3rd Earl of Lichfield, as a Boy* (1856–1918)
Brown ink, signed
Drawn in 1863 when Landseer was staying at Shugborough.

ON CABINET

49 *Louisa, Duchess of Abercorn and her daughter Harriet*
Sir Edwin Landseer, RA (1802–73)
Slate, signed and dated 1834
Lady Louisa Russell (1812–1905), second daughter of the 6th Duke of Bedford, married the 1st Duke of Abercorn in 1832. Lady Harriet Hamilton married the 2nd Earl of Lichfield in 1855.

106 *Four Animal Studies*
Sir Edwin Landseer, RA (1802–73)
Pencil, on one mount, two signed and dated 1845
See note for Nos. 102–5.

The State Bedroom

STATE BEDROOM

107 *2nd Earl of Lichfield* (1825–92)
Anton Solom calling himself Anthony de Salomé
(fl. second half of nineteenth century)
Coloured chalks, signed and dated 1860

108 *Lady Harriet Hamilton, Countess of Lichfield*
(d.1913)
Sir Edwin Landseer, RA (1802–73)
Coloured chalks

109 *Lady Louisa Russell, Duchess of Abercorn*
(1812–1905)
Anton Solom, calling himself Anthony de Salomé
(fl. second half of nineteenth century)
Coloured chalks, signed and dated 1860

110 *Lady Georgiana Hamilton, Countess of Winterton*
(d.1913)
Anton Solom, calling himself Anthony de Salomé
(fl. second half of nineteenth century)
Coloured chalks, signed and dated 1860
Fifth daughter of the 1st Duke of Abercorn and wife
of the 5th Earl of Winterton.

THE SALOON

Back on the ground floor, a door leads from the end of the Swallow Passage into the Saloon in the centre of the west front. This occupies the site of Thomas Anson's dining-room. The room was doubled in size and totally remodelled by Samuel Wyatt between 1803 and 1806, some ten years after his other alterations to the house and said to be in preparation for a visit from the Prince Regent which never materialised. It gave the house a large central place of assembly, made particularly necessary by the small size of the entrance hall. On the exterior, the effect of this room jutting out beyond the rest of the building is not altogether happy, but, inside, the rows of giant yellow scagliola columns reflected in the tall pier glasses at the east end give an exaggerated sense of perspective that is extremely impressive. The columns and their dosserets (or the detached sections of entablature which they support) were supplied by Joseph Alcott, and the plaster capitals by Francis Bernasconi. The latter are very accurate copies of the simplified Corinthian order employed on the Tower of the Winds in Athens and published by Stuart in *The Antiquities of Athens*. Wyatt's use of them here illustrates his aim to maintain the pure Greek quality of the architecture at Shugborough.

The inner of the two chimney-pieces uses the old flue of the Georgian dining-room, but in order to balance it and keep the symmetry of the room, Wyatt provided a second, further to the west. The white marble surrounds with metal inlay are the work of Charles Rossi (1762–1839), who had been appointed sculptor to the Prince of Wales in 1797. The ceiling may originally have been plain as now, but Amadée Joubert substituted some rather half-hearted decorative panels in 1899; these were in turn removed about 1920.

FURNITURE

The mahogany single chairs, *bergères*, sofas and footstools with ormolu mounts, were supplied by Charles Smith & Co. and form part of the original furnishing of the room. At the same time the pair of mahogany side tables near the windows, which date from about 1760, were given ormolu mounts and new marble tops designed by Samuel Wyatt to match the rest of the furniture. The pier tables and glasses were supplied by Morant & Boyd for the 2nd Earl of Lichfield in 1853, together with the curtains and the red plush upholstery of Smith's chairs and sofas. The mahogany and kingwood *bureau plat* in the window bay is French of the Louis XV period. On it stands a large scale model of the Egyptian obelisk known as Constantine's Column, in ormolu. On the tables and the two chimney-pieces are a number of Louis XVI and Empire bronze and ormolu candelabra, and two Parisian clocks of about 1780. The pair of large English Majolica vases with entwined snake handles were made in Stoke-on-Trent in the nineteenth century and are signed 'T. Kirkby'. The Turkey carpet is English c.1890 and from the County Buildings, Stafford.

PICTURES

The portraits here include those of Admiral Lord Anson, painted in 1755, and Mary Vernon, mother of the 1st Viscount, both by Sir Joshua Reynolds.

38 *Daniel Cunyngham* (b.1701)
Mason Chamberlin, RA (1727–87)
Inscribed on reverse and dated 1766
Nothing appears to be known about the sitter, but his portrayal in seventeenth-century dress suggests that he may have been a friend of Thomas Anson's who shared the same antiquarian tastes.

39 *Mary Vernon, Mrs Anson*
Sir Joshua Reynolds, PRA (1723–92)
Painted in 1764
Daughter of George, 1st Lord Vernon, and wife of George Adams, who changed his name to Anson on inheriting Shugborough from his uncle, Thomas Anson.

40 *Admiral Sir Charles Saunders* (?1713–75)
After Sir Joshua Reynolds, PRA (1723–92)
A modern copy of the original of 1765 by Reynolds, at one time at Shugborough and now in the National Maritime Museum, Greenwich. Sir Charles Saunders, who accompanied Anson on his voyage in 1740, was 1st Lord of the Admiralty in 1766.

41 *Lady Elizabeth Yorke, Lady Anson* (d.1760)
Studio of Thomas Hudson (1701–79)
Daughter of 1st Earl of Hardwicke and wife of Admiral Lord Anson, whom she married in 1748. For another portrait see No. 43.

42 *Admiral Lord Anson* (1697–1762)
Sir Joshua Reynolds, PRA (1723–92)
Painted in 1755
The portrait, which had been presented to Sir Piercy Brett, one of Anson's officers, passed by descent to Sir George Bowyer. After the sale of Sir George's paintings in 1871, it was bought by the 3rd Earl of Lichfield.

43 *Lady Elizabeth Yorke, Lady Anson* (d.1760)
(?) John Vanderbank (1694–1739)
See No. 41, where she appears as an older woman.

THE VERANDAH ROOM AND PASSAGE

This was formed in 1911 by the architect H. L. Anderson, by amalgamating two rooms and a passage in order to make the more commodious billiard room required by Edwardian country-house life. The alterations were done sympathetically to match the Georgian character of the house. The Rococo plasterwork ceiling from the Chinese House had already been moved here in 1885 for safety. Again likely to be the work of Vassalli in about 1747, its design and execution are of the highest quality, using chinoiserie motifs but in a controlled Italianate composition. The four jolly figures of mandarins in the corner medallions have particular charm. The neo-Classical chimney-piece was probably brought from elsewhere in the house by the 3rd Earl, and the early eighteenth-century Boulle bracket clock in the passage is signed by 'J. Godde, l'aîné, à Paris'.

FURNITURE AND CERAMICS

The mahogany display cabinet is filled with the famous armorial service of nearly 200 pieces, presented to Admiral Lord Anson by the European merchants of Canton in recognition of the part played by the crew of the *Centurion* in extinguishing a fire that threatened the city. The design in the centre is unique and the scene is based on an original drawing done by Piercy Brett which later formed the basis for the illustrations of Tinian Island (Plate XXXIV) in Anson's *Voyage*, published in 1748. The bread-fruit tree and palm sustained the crew when marooned on Tinian Island, while the faithful dogs, altar of love and shepherds' pipes speak of thoughts of home. On the rim are views of Plymouth Sound, the Pearl River, and the Eddystone and Macao lighthouses. At the top is the Anson crest, and at the bottom the Anson arms quartering Carrier (the mother of George and Thomas Anson being an heraldic heiress).

More china is displayed in the vitrines on either side of the fireplace. Of particular note is the Wedgwood Queen's Ware cream bowl decorated with a view of Shugborough Park, including the Triumphal Arch, a view near Richmond Castle and two scenes near Ludlow Castle. It is either a trial piece for the celebrated Green Frog Service supplied by Wedgwood to the Empress Catherine II of Russia in 1774, or a special order made after it. While some of the scenes were copied from prints, others, including the view of Shugborough, were painted from life.

Other good pieces include a Meissen tea and coffee service painted in a Watteauesque manner, a Naples *écuelle* with gilt griffin finial and a pair of blue jasper ware jardinières made by Wedgwood in 1782 for the father of the 1st Viscount Anson.

The furniture includes a Louis XVI parquetry jardinière, bearing the stamp of the maker Ferdinand Bury, registered as a *maître-ébéniste* in Paris in 1774.

A particularly interesting relic is the lion's leg in carved wood mounted on a mahogany shield-shaped plaque in the passage. This is all that survives of the lion figurehead of Admiral Anson's ship, HMS *Centurion*. It had a chequered history before reaching Shugborough. When the ship was broken up, George III gave the figurehead, which then stood 16 feet high, to the Duke of Richmond, Master-General of the Ordnance. The Duke placed it on a pedestal to serve as a pub sign at Waterbeach on his estate at Goodwood. There it was spotted by William IV who begged it and placed it for a time on the Grand Staircase at Windsor Castle. Later he presented it to Greenwich Hospital where it embellished the Anson Ward, until banished to an outhouse after falling into disrepair. Capt. W. V. Anson, Admiral Anson's biographer, tracked down the remaining leg at the beginning of this century and gave it to the 3rd Earl of Lichfield who was keenly interested in the family history.

In the passage is part of a set of prefabricated Chinese Huang Hua Li armchairs. They date from the early eighteenth century and were brought back to England by the Admiral.

PICTURES

The large collection of paintings of horses and fox-hounds commemorates the 1st Earl's love of hunting and racing and is mostly by William Webb and Thomas Weaver, though *Elis*, which won the St Leger in 1836, also appears in pictures by J. F. Herring and Henry Alken.

The continuation of the Verandah Room passage, leading to the private staircase at the south end of the house, is hung with a unique series of fifteen water-colours of the house, the park and monuments at Shugborough by Moses Griffith, all commissioned by the topographer Thomas Pennant and dating from about 1780. They were bought by the 4th Earl of Lichfield when Pennant's library was sold in 1938.

Here, too, are four finished studies by Dall for his oil paintings seen elsewhere in the house.

PASSAGE FROM HALL

44 *Two Dogs and a dead Pheasant*
William Webb (1780–1846)
Signed and dated 1822

45 *The West Front of Shugborough*
Nicholas Dall, ARA (fl.1756–d.1776)
Signed and dated 1768
The house is seen before the upper storey was added to the link buildings (*cf.* No. 66). The ruined temple is on the near bank of the River Sow with Ruins, Orangery and Chinese House on the far side.

46 *A Longhorn Cow and Farm Labourer*
James Ward, RA (1769–1859)
Panel, monogrammed
The name of the farm labourer was Jerry Hudson.

Wedgwood cream bowl decorated with a view of Shugborough Park

47 *A Shooting Party at Ranton Abbey*
Sir Francis Grant, PRA (1810–78)
Painted in 1840. The 1st Earl of Lichfield is mounted on a white pony, with Lord Melbourne on his right and Lord Uxbridge behind him, wearing a grey hat. Lord Sefton is seated at the left; the boy lying on the ground is Lord Anson. Ranton Abbey is a Lichfield property in Staffordshire.

MAIN SECTION OF ROOM

75 *A chestnut Hunter saddled outside a Stable*
William Webb (1780–1846)
Signed

76 *A Groom and bay Hunter outside Shugborough*
William Webb (1780–1846)
Signed and dated 1822

77 *A Foxhound Bitch and Litter*
William Webb (1780–1846)
Signed and dated 1823
Pair to No. 79.

78 *'Rose' and a Portuguese Horse*
Thomas Weaver (1774–1843)
Signed and dated 1811
Lady Anson's favourite mare and the 1st Viscount's horse.
Pair to No. 80.

79 *Foxhounds in Kennels*
William Webb (1780–1846)
Signed and dated 1823
Pair to No. 77.

80 *'Snowdrop and Nimble'*
Thomas Weaver (1774–1843)
Signed and dated 1811
Pair to No. 78.

81 *A bay Hunter in a Loose Box*
William Webb (1780–1846)
Signed and dated 1823

82 *A bay Hunter in Shugborough Park*
William Webb (1780–1846)

83 *Corsican Goat's Head*
Thomas Weaver (1774–1843)
Signed and dated 1808
Thomas Anson kept a herd of Corsican goats, which Sir Joseph Banks observed on a visit to Shugborough in 1768.
Pair to No. 87.

84 *Elis*
J. F. Herring (1795–1865)
Signed and dated 1836
Trained by the 1st Earl, the horse won the St Leger in 1836. The jockey is J. Day.

85 *The Stables at Shugborough with a bay Hunter*
William Webb (1780–1846)
Signed and dated 1824

86 *Thomas Coke, 1st Earl of Leicester* (1752–1842)
R. R. Reinagle (1775–1863)
Signed and dated 1815
His daughter Anne married the 1st Viscount Anson. In the background is Holkham, Norfolk.

87 *Corsican Goat's Head*
Thomas Weaver (1774–1843)
Signed and dated 1808
Pair to No. 83.

88 *A chestnut Hunter saddled for a Lady*
Thomas Weaver (1774–1843)
Signed and dated 1808

89 *A brown Horse in a Landscape*
Thomas Weaver (1774–1843)
Signed and dated 1808

90 *'Elis' beating Colonel Peel's 'Slane'*
Henry Alken (1771–1850)
Signed and dated 1837
The race was run at Newmarket in 1837 for 300 guineas. Elis was the first horse for whom a horse box was made.

FAR SECTION OF PASSAGE

55–74 Drawings of Shugborough

The series of watercolour drawings by Moses Griffith was done in about 1780, after the link buildings had been increased in height but before the house was altered by Samuel Wyatt. Those by Dall are finished studies for the oil paintings of 1768 and 1775 in the house.

55 *The Lanthorn of Demosthenes*
Moses Griffith (1747–1819).

56 *An extensive View of the Park and Monuments*
Nicholas Dall, ARA (fl.1756–d.1776)
The wooden obelisk, situated on Brocton Hill, blew down in the nineteenth century. By 1752 the skeleton of the Pagoda was up and 'promising greatly'. Thus it anticipated the Pagoda executed by Sir William Chambers at Kew. The Pagoda, Cascade and Palladian Bridge had disappeared by 1800, perhaps through the great floods of 1795; the pool was probably drained shortly afterwards, at the time the alternative channel was cut for the River Sow. An item 'Work done [on the] new river' is included in an account totalling £9,541 3s 9¾d submitted by 'Mr. Webb, Landscape Gardener' for work upon the grounds at Shugborough, 1798–1805. A preparatory study for No. 33.

57–60 Moses Griffith (1747–1819).

57 *The Triumphal Arch.*

58 *The East Front of Shugborough*
Signed. *Cf.* No. 62
The Essex Bridge is in the foreground.

59 *A Classical Statue* (?Tragedy)
This and No. 63 occupied the niches at either end of
the Orangery.

60 *The Lanthorn of Demosthenes.*

61 *Oakedge*
Nicholas Dall, ARA (fl.1756–d.1776)
A preparatory study for No. 3.

62–67 Moses Griffith (1747–1819).

62 *The East Front of Shugborough*
Seen from a greater distance than No. 58, with the
Arch of Hadrian in the background.

63 *A Classical Statue* (?Oratory).

64 *The East Front of Shugborough*
An oblique view, with the Arch of Hadrian in the
distance.

65 *The Palladian Bridge and Cascade.*

66 *The West Front of Shugborough*
Seen across the River Sow, with the Ruins and
Orangery.

67 *The Tower of the Winds*
Signed

68 *The West Front of Shugborough*
Nicholas Dall, ARA (fl.1756–d.1776)
The Ruins are in the foreground; beyond them is the
Greenhouse or Orangery, about the enlargement of
which Stuart corresponded with Anson in 1764. It
was demolished *c.*1855. A partial preparatory study
for No. 45.

69 *The Chinese House*
Moses Griffith (1747–1819)

70 *An extensive View of the Park and Monument*
Moses Griffith (1747–1819)
Almost identical to No. 56 by Dall.

71 *The Ruins*
Nicholas Dall, ARA (fl.1756–d.1776)
A preparatory study for No. 2.

72 *The Palladian Bridge and Cascade*
Edward Jones(?–?)
Inscribed: *A view at Mr Anson's Seat in Staffordshire by
Edwd Jones.*

73 *The Tower of the Winds*
Moses Griffith (1747–1819)
A more distant view than No. 67.

74 *The West Front of Shugborough*
Moses Griffith (1747–1819)

THE LIBRARY

Writing in 1748 of recent improvements at Shugborough, Lady Grey reported that 'the house had
some fine rooms lately added to it, and one exceedingly odd and pretty that is the Library'; so the room
can be dated to that period, and attributed, like the
Dining Room, to the architect Thomas Wright of
Durham. It consists of two parts: one half of it is
contained in the central block of the house; the other
is in the link to the south pavilion. They are joined
by a flattened arch burrowed through the thickness
of the outer wall of the old house. The arch is 5 feet
deep and only 8 feet high owing to the lowness of
the ceiling, and is carried on small Ionic columns and
pillars.

The apparent length of the whole room – actually
less than 40 feet – is increased by the perspective of
the arch, by the further part being slightly narrower,
and by the mirrors placed at the side of the columns
which give the illusion of continuous bookshelves
behind them. The chimney-piece, using the already
existing flue from the old house, is considerably off-
centre, which gives a subtly telling touch of
irregularity.

The bookcases with arched recesses above them in
the northern half of the room are thought to be
original, while those with pediments in the southern
section are again slightly later additions. According
to a letter from James Stuart in 1770, one wall of the
Library was then being painted by Dall, perhaps the
recess which now contains a bookcase at the southern
end.

The Rococo plasterwork decoration must again be
the work of Vassalli. In the ceilings are two large
central reliefs of Fame and Minerva, the former
surrounded by medallions of philosophers, the latter
by trophies representing the arts and sciences, and
reflecting Thomas Anson's own predilections. The
two medallions on the wall to the left of the chimney-piece represent *The Three Graces* and *Apollo and
Daphne* after Bernini, testifying also to his love of
Italian painting and sculpture. It is unfortunate that
so many of Thomas Anson's books were dispersed in
the sale of 1842. He appears to have been particularly
interested in archaeology and architecture – unsur-

The Library

prising tastes, perhaps. What remains is not entirely insignificant and includes a fine set of Diderot's *Encyclopédie* and what is probably the Admiral's own copy of his *Voyage round the World*.

FURNITURE AND SCULPTURE

The marble busts which surmount the bookshelves range from the antique – including Hercules, Plato and Tiberius Caesar – to nineteenth-century portraits of members of the family, among them the 1st Countess of Lichfield seen holding a rabbit, to the right of the pediment on the west wall. The niches set between the Ionic pillars of the arch contain busts of the 6th Duke of Bedford by Nollekens, 1803, and Coke of Norfolk by George Garrard, 1806.

The furniture is mostly early nineteenth century, and includes more of the set of mahogany chairs by

Charles Smith & Co. seen in the Saloon. The small mahogany sofa table is of a type associated with Gillows of Lancaster, with its characteristic star-shaped mounts to the drawer handles. The pair of vases on the mantelpiece, decorated in imitation of tortoiseshell and mounted in ormolu, are Sèvres.

PICTURES

ON EASEL

50 *Viscount Coke and the Hon. Edward Coke*
Samuel Lane (1780–1859)
Two children of the 1st Earl of Leicester by his second wife, Lady Anne Keppel; the elder succeeded as 2nd Earl in 1842.

N.B. On the jambs of the door to the Anson Room may be seen the pencilled heights of successive generations of Anson children.

THE ANSON ROOM

This room was redecorated in 1983 by David Mlinaric as a withdrawing room and is used by the Earl of Lichfield. It contains a large number of relics and mementoes of Admiral Lord Anson. These include: his gold repeating watch by George Graham, with a dial engraved by G. M. Moser, c.1740; his snuff box; the seal box given to him with the freedom of the City of Plymouth; his commission from George II as Admiral of the Blue; wood from his cabin in HMS *Centurion*; medals commemorating his circumnavigation, together with versions of these in Wedgwood pottery; and many prints. Beneath the large oil painting hangs the silver mounted sword surrendered to him by the vanquished Spanish commander of the treasure galleon. The Spanish coins also came from the same source. His commission of appointment as Admiral of the United Kingdom is framed in wood from the figurehead of the *Centurion*.

FURNITURE

The furniture includes a fine satinwood bookcase of c.1800 by Gillows of Lancaster. The satinwood *secrétaire* commode was made by the same firm.

PICTURES

53 *Admiral Lord Anson* (1697–1762)
William Hoare, RA (1702–92)
Pastel
Probably drawn about 1750, he is wearing Flag Officer's undress uniform.

54 *The Capture of the 'Nuestra Señora de Covadonga'*
John Cleveley (fl.1726–77)
Signed and dated 1756
Commodore Anson in the *Centurion* attacking the Spanish treasure galleon off the Philippine Islands on 20 April 1743. This was bought in at the 1842 sale by the estate agent Harvey Wyatt.

THE BOUDOIR
(Open occasionally)

This charming small room is among the best preserved at Shugborough. The grey moiré wallpaper
with cut-out floral border was supplied by Eckhardt
in 1794 and is the only one of their papers to survive
in the house. The bow, cornice and chimney-piece
are by Samuel Wyatt but the doorcase with carved
entablature dates from the mid-eighteenth century
and survives from Thomas Anson's work. The Eckhardt brothers, of Chelsea, were the leading manu-
facturers of wallpaper in England in the late eighteenth and early nineteenth centuries. Anthony
George and Francis Frederick Eckhardt are thought
to have come to London from Holland in the early
1770s. In 1774 Anthony George, who had recently
been elected a Fellow of the Royal Society, took out
a patent 'for printing designs on silk, cotton, muslins,
calicos and paper'. A further patent taken out by
Francis Frederick in 1793 was 'for Preparing and
Printing Paper in different patterns and to silver it
over with Fine Silver leaves so as to resemble
Damask, Lace and Various Silk Stuffs to be used for
Hangings and other Furniture for Rooms'. The
papers supplied to Shugborough in the 1790s were
manufactured according to this patent, and that in
this boudoir is one of the finest early Eckhardt papers
to survive.

CHAPTER SEVEN

GARDEN AND PARK

THE GARDEN

Only traces of Thomas Anson's mid-eighteenth-century Rococo layout have survived nineteenth-century remodelling and twentieth-century re-planting. Lying immediately to the west of the house is now a series of formal terraced lawns, with clipped golden yews and stone urns laid out *c*.1855 under the direction of the landscape gardener W. A. Nesfield. In the 1960s the terraces were planted in a theme of yellow, purple and grey, and recently the rose beds have been replanted with the yellow floribunda rose 'Bright Smile'. The border in front of the office wing is planted with Buddleia, *Hosta ventricosa* 'Variegata', *Brunnera macrophylla*, *Cornus alba* 'Elegantissima', shrubby potentillas and *Hydrangea paniculata*. At the east end can be found a pair of lion columns from a temple in South India, thought to date from around AD 800.

The lawns occupy the site of Thomas Anson's bowling green and step gently down to the River Sow beside which are situated the Ruins. They are at least in part the work of Thomas Wright. Originally they were far more extensive, stretching westwards and including a Gothic pigeon house. They were composed of parts of the old house, pulled down for the addition of the bow to the west front, and fragments of the former palace of the Bishops of Lichfield. On the opposite bank of the river stood a Classical colonnade, possibly an adaptation of the Temple of Saturn in the Roman Forum, which disappeared probably at the time of the Great Flood in 1795.

Seated on a rubble crag are the remains of a Druid, made from Coade stone. In the eighteenth-century pictures of the Ruin, the Druid contrasts markedly in colour with the rest of the structure. The whole monument was sadly neglected for many years and in the 1960s was found to be leaning badly towards the river. In order to correct this, the east side was excavated to re-establish it in an upright position. The balustrade and entablature had been damaged by the penetration of ivy roots, and so in 1969 it was recommended that the growth and bushes from around the monument be removed and the roots killed, but the silver birches were left as these appeared in the paintings of the original composition. The monument was brushed down and the joints tamped and pointed, farther from the face than usual to retain the ruined effect. The figure was cleaned and repainted, and the broken balustrading fixed with non-ferrous metal dowels. The small pond with a fountain in the form of a lead statue of a boy and swan was added *c*.1900.

To the south is the Wild Garden which occupies the site of Thomas Anson's shrubbery and is at its best in spring when the daffodils are out, and in late May and early June when the rhododendrons are in flower. The trees include holly, lime, sweet and horse chestnut, oak, beech, the Swedish birch (*Betula pendula* 'Laciniata') and cut leaf alder. There are glimpses across the park to the Tower of the Winds and the Lanthorn of Demosthenes (see pp.85–90). At the end is the Blue Bridge, erected in cast iron in 1813 by Charles Heywood. It leads across the River Sow to the Arboretum established in the nineteenth century and containing various interesting trees, including Wellingtonias and the present Lord Lichfield's unique collection of different varieties of oak trees.

Retracing steps back past the house, the North Walk is reached. This path forms part of Thomas Anson's layout, and its original state was serpentine and gravelled with wide grass verges and flanking beds of shrubs and rare trees interspersed with antique sculpture. It leads to the Chinese House, completed in 1747 and probably the first of Thomas Anson's garden buildings.

The design for the Chinese House was taken from the pencil sketches of Sir Piercy Brett, Admiral Anson's second-in-command on the *Centurion*. It must have been constructed shortly after the Admiral's return, making it one of the earliest buildings of Chinese influence in the country, a precursor of the Chinese 'Pavilion' at Kew. The watercolour by Moses Griffith, 1780, shows the outside of the Chinese House looking very similar to its present appearance but coloured pale blue and white. The colour scheme within survives, with its pale green canopy, gilt monkeys and alcoves with red lacquer fretwork and gilded details.

The Chinese House was built on an island in an artificial canal, with a boathouse attached. It was reached by a pair of bridges of Chinese design. This arrangement was altered during the rerouting of the Sow after the flooding of 1795 which left the Chinese House standing on a little promontory with only one bridge, rebuilt in iron, leading to the newly made island. The bridge, painted a bright Chinese red, was erected in 1813 by Charles Heywood.

In 1885 the contents of the Chinese House, the plaster ceiling, four painted mirror pictures, fret tables, rushbottom chairs and porcelain were removed to the house for safekeeping.

The planting hereabouts in Thomas Anson's day

Terraced lawns to the west of the house

The Ruins

included clumps of larches, known as 'Indian Trees', but these have all disappeared. Nevertheless, the planting round the Chinese House is still deliberately oriental in feel, with tree peonies, bamboo, azaleas, *Viburnum davidi*, *Osmanthus delavayi*, *Rodgersia aesculifolia*, *Ligustrum quihoui* and *Ligustrum lucidum*.

Situated on the island which lies between the old and new channels of the River Sow, is the Cat's Monument. This was conceived in about 1749 and was probably designed by Thomas Wright. Two hypotheses lie behind the purpose of this monu-

ment. One is that it commemorates a cat which travelled around the world with Admiral Anson in the *Centurion*; the other, more probable, that it is a memorial to the Persian cat kept for many years by Thomas Anson called 'Kouli-Khun'.

Thomas also kept a herd of Corsican goats, which figure around the base of the monument, and can be seen in the paintings by Thomas Weaver (Nos. 83 and 87) in the Verandah Room. Both cat and goats were recorded as having been seen by Sir Joseph Banks in 1768. He noted that Thomas Anson had kept a breed of Persian cats 'for many years, but one

The Cat's Monument. It commemorates a Persian cat kept by Thomas Anson called 'Kouli-Khun'

is now left, all the rest having died of a distemper'. The back of the monument is of rough stonework because it was built against a large beech tree which has since died. The tablet on the front is of Coade stone and is a later addition, probably of the 1770s. The design of a pair of griffins flanking a vase is derived from an engraving in Antoine Desgodetz's *Les Edifices Antiques de Rome* (Paris, 1682). Before the trees grew up, blocking the view, the Cat's Monument would have faced, across the river, the Shepherd's Monument.

Back on the mainland and continuing along the riverside path past plantings of *Viburnum plicatum* var. *tomentosum* and *Parrotia persica*, the Shepherd's Monument is reached on the right. When built, this backed onto the outside of the old kitchen garden wall and was not free-standing as it is now. It was already in existence by 1758 and was probably built c.1750. It was designed by Thomas Wright and takes its name from the marble relief sculpture. The rough hewn arch into which this is inserted bears a striking resemblance to the first of Thomas Wright's *Six Original Designs for Arbours* published in 1755. The primitive columns and Doric entablature with crestings were probably added in 1763 by James Stuart.

The monument takes its name from the marble relief, based on an engraving of the painting by Nicolas Poussin, *Et in Arcadia Ego* (1640–2). This was carved by Peter Scheemakers. Pennant describes it:

The scene is laid in Arcadia. Two lovers, expressed in elegant pastoral figures, appear attentive to an ancient shepherd, who reads to them an inscription on the tomb, Et in Arcadia Ego! The moral resulting from this seems to be that there are no situations of life so delicious, but which death must at length snatch us from. It was placed here by the amiable owner, as a memento of the certainty of that event. Perhaps also as a secret memorial of some loss of a tender nature in his early days, for he was wont often to hang over it in affectionate and firm meditation.

On a tablet below the relief is a cryptic inscription, the cause of much inconclusive speculation:

$$\text{D.} \quad ^{O\ U\ O\ S\ V\ A\ V\ V} \quad \text{M.}$$

It has been suggested that the D.M. stands either as initials or for the Latin 'Dis Manibus'. This was found commonly on Roman tombs, dedicating the soul of one departed to the spirit world, although in this case they do not stand together.

Beyond is the famous Shugborough Yew Tree, reputedly the largest in England, its spread having a circumference of 525 feet. At charity garden parties between the wars, an admission charge was made and special tickets issued for visiting the tree.

At the end of the walk is a glimpse beyond the edge of the park of the sixteenth-century Essex Bridge spanning the combined waters of the rivers Sow and Trent.

Turning back towards the house, The Flat is reached, an expanse of lawn and evergreen shrubs overlooked by the Doric Temple. This hexastyle* portico was almost certainly designed by James Stuart and was conceived as the entrance to the kitchen garden, which at that time occupied the space between it and the Shepherd's Monument. The present uncomfortably truncated and isolated appearance of the temple is the result of the demolition of the old walled garden in 1805. There is no documentary evidence to support the attribution to Stuart, but it is so close in appearance to the Temple designed by him at Hagley in 1758, and reputed to be the first accurate revived Greek Doric Temple in Europe, as to make it highly likely that Stuart was responsible. They are both based on the Temple of Hephaistos, known commonly as the Theseion, and dedicated to Athena, which crowns the hill overlooking the Agora in Athens (449–444 BC). The original was situated in a garden, hence its appropriateness as the portico leading to the site of the walled garden at Shugborough. The south side of the garden was screened by Thomas Anson's orangery, but this was demolished c.1855 when Nesfield's terrace was laid out. The sculpture which it contained had been sold in 1842, and the structure had probably deteriorated during the 1st Earl's sojourn abroad.

The site of the orangery has been laid out as a Rose Garden to the original design of Graham Stuart Thomas. The intention has been to create a

* with a portico of six columns.

The Rose Garden

Victorian atmosphere and the formal beds are planted with appropriate old-type roses, including polyantha, climber and shrub roses. The finely carved eighteenth-century marble urn is a survivor from Thomas Anson's collection and is attributed to Peter Scheemakers.

THE STABLES

To the left of the entrance front, and set back behind a belt of trees, is the mid-eighteenth-century stable block, built of brick with stone dressings, a cupola above the central archway. The clock and bell are of 1767, which may also be the date of the whole block. The architect of this unpretentious building is not known, but could well have been the local master-mason, Charles Cope Trubshaw of Haywood, who executed Stuart's Temple of the Winds and other monuments in the park in the 1760s. The elaborate pedimented window frame or aedicule, with Doric columns on the end wall of the neighbouring coach-house, originally came from one of Thomas Wright's one-storey links between the central block of the house and the two 'pavilions'. It was presumably removed to this position in 1794, when displaced by one of Samuel Wyatt's tripartite windows.

The Dormeuse Travelling Chariot in the coach-house was used for long-distance travel in Britain and on the Continent. The body extends into the front boot to enable the occupants to sleep full-length on long journeys (hence 'dormeuse'). The original leather-covered trunks or 'imperials' are still in place. This superb example was built by Adams & Co., Haymarket, London. It can be dated c.1825–30.

The stables now contain the Staffordshire County Museum, with displays devoted to local social history and rural life, a collection of carriages in the old coach-house, and the kitchen, butler's pantry and the laundry in the office wing maintained in working order as they would have been in the nineteenth century. In the midden yard are grown the blue sweet peas 'Admiral Anson' (*Lathyrus nervosus*), descendants of those seeds which Lord Anson's cook is reputed to have brought back from Juan Fernandez.

Under the trees in front of the stables is a dogs' graveyard instituted in 1910 with little memorial stones to Anson pets.

THE PARK

The Park at Shugborough, quite apart from its intrinsic natural beauty, has an importance all its own, for the temples and monuments dotted about it form a landmark in the evolution of English eighteenth-century architecture. In 1755 James Stuart and his companion Nicholas Revett returned from Greece where they had spent several years studying and measuring the remains of Hellenic buildings. In 1762 the first volume of their long-awaited *The Antiquities of Athens* was published in London. The book caused an immense stir in architectural circles, and it launched a new vogue for the Greek taste, which was to run parallel with the Roman and the 'Gothick' and endure for at least a hundred years. At Shugborough, Thomas Anson commissioned Stuart to construct a three-dimensional version of the *Antiquities* in his park.

The Doric Temple referred to above and the monuments about to be described are among the very first buildings in England in the neo-Greek style. Small though they are in size, their interest is therefore considerable.

TOWER OF THE WINDS

This reproduction of the Horlogium of Andronikos Cyrrhestes in Athens was executed by Charles Cope Trubshaw of Haywood under the direction of Stuart and must have been completed about 1765, when James and Thomas Warreley, plumbers, inscribed their names on the leadwork to the roof. The original Tower on which it is modelled has in the frieze deep sculptured reliefs of the Winds and no windows. The Moses Griffith drawing of the Tower at Shugborough, reproduced in Pennant's *Journey from Chester to London* (1782), shows reproductions of the Winds reliefs and windows in the upper storey only. However, ground-floor windows are depicted in Moses Griffith's watercolours in the Verandah Passage and in one of Dall's paintings. Sculptural reliefs were never put up, although it may be that they were merely painted.

The lower two storeys were converted into a dairy for Lady Anson by Samuel Wyatt *c.*1805.

The interior of the Tower of the Winds has recently been restored by the National Trust. The ground-floor room is lined with Derbyshire alabaster and has stained glass in the windows. Round the sides are marble shelves for the milk pans and other dairy pots. The last comprise a splendid set in black and terracotta earthenware with Egyptian decoration; they were provided by Wedgwood. They are now stored in the house for safe-keeping. The basement room was the 'scalding room' for the dairy, where the dairy utensils were washed in hot water. This room is lined with Penrhyn slate and the shelves along the side and the table in the centre are also of slate. A spiral staircase leads up to 'Athenian' Stuart's first-floor 'Banqueting Room'. Note the little stoup or basin for washing hands, set into the newel on the way up. Stuart's decoration in the first-floor room was reinstated in 1987–8 following detailed analysis of the paint layers. The chimney-piece (found in store) has been put back, and the carved architraves, window shutters and other joinery are copies from the originals. The beautiful

(*Left*) The Tower of the Winds

(*Facing page*) Ceiling of the Tower of the Winds

coffered ceiling survived the late nineteenth-century dismantling of the rest of the room and is based on the design of one in Nero's 'Golden House' in Rome.

From the windows, there were good views over the park in all directions. Originally the Tower of the Winds stood at the end of Thomas Anson's lake and faced the Palladian Bridge and the Chinese Pagoda. But that part of the original layout disappeared during the 1st Viscount's scheme of further improvements in the late eighteenth and early nineteenth centuries. The Tower now reads as an appendage to Park Farm.

PARK FARM

The present farm buildings were designed by Samuel Wyatt and built in 1805 for Viscount Anson as the home farm of the estate. The land had been farmed from White Barn Farm, but the early nineteenth century saw the creation of many purpose-built farms planned for efficient management, incorporating modern machinery and up-to-date techniques. Landowners of the time vied with one another to build such 'model' farms, and Shugborough Park Farm was considered extremely modern. Viscount Anson was a progressive farmer possibly because of the influence, through his wife, of the famous agricultural improver Thomas Coke, Earl of Leicester, of Holkham in Norfolk; like Coke, Viscount Anson was advised by Nathaniel Kent, the first modern consultant estate agent who also planned the farms in Windsor Great Park for George III.

The buildings form a quadrangle of red brick and, according to William Pitt in his *Topographical History of Staffordshire*, consisted in 1817 of:

Farming steward's house on one side: a range of buildings on another contains a brewhouse, upon a large scale, a water cornmill for the use of the family and farm, and in which corn is ground for the neighbouring poor gratis, and also a malt-house. The opposite side and end are occupied by stalls for feeding cattle, store-rooms, stables and other appendages. In the middle of the yard is a very complete hoggery, built of large stones set edgewise and covered with slate.

A later description in 1835 also mentions a dovecot, slaughterhouse, poultry houses, dairy and a pleasure ground adjacent to the Bailiff's house, although the hoggery, dovecot and poultry houses have now disappeared. Today the farm is run as an agricultural museum by the County Council.

White Barn, situated half a mile to the south east of the main agricultural complex in the park, was the original farm created by Thomas Anson to serve his sheep walks and arable enclosures on the slopes of Cannock Chase.

THE KITCHEN GARDEN

The Walled Garden was designed by Samuel Wyatt and built at about the same period as the farm, 1805–6, to replace the old kitchen garden. William Pitt gave a detailed description in 1817:

A kitchen garden of several acres is walled and subdivided; the walls well stocked with the choicest fruit trees, with very extensive ranges of hot-houses, in which the pineapple, the grape, the peach, the fig, and other varieties of hot-house fruits, flowers and plants are cultivated in the highest perfection. One of the hot-houses is heated with steam, in which melons and cucumbers are produced in perfection at all seasons. These gardens are a kind of Academy for the study of Horticulture, in which young men enter themselves to assist without pay, for the purpose of improving themselves, and gaining knowledge in the art.

The area continued to be used as the kitchen garden until the 1950s, but is now devoted to other uses. The high encircling brick walls survive.

The eastern part of the park formed the second phase of Thomas Anson's improvements in the mid-eighteenth century, and involved the enclosure of a thousand acres of the manorial waste on the slopes of Cannock Chase. This area was at first separated from the 'home park' by the main Stafford–Rugeley road, but Viscount Anson's diversion of the road to its present line made it all one uninterrupted large-scale layout. This area was intended as sheep pasture enlivened with circular clumps of mixed trees: Scots pine, larch, beech and chestnut. The original intention was that some of the clumps should be open and others fenced in and underplanted with laurels and evergreens.

The Lanthorn of Demosthenes (Choragic Monument of Lysicrates)

BIBLIOGRAPHY

MANUSCRIPT SOURCES

The Anson family and Estate Papers are deposited in the Staffordshire Record Office (D615/E[H]).

The Anson Letters, a collection of papers relating to Admiral Lord Anson, are in the Department of Manuscripts at the British Library.

Lesser Manuscript sources include:

Westminster City Library, Gillow MSS, 902,1152.

British Library, Hardwicke MSS.

Bedford Record Office, Grey MSS L30/9a/2/3–32 (correspondence of Jemima, Marchioness Grey).

Cambridge University Library, 'Sir Joseph Banks' Journal of an Excursion into Wales' (Add. MS. 6294).

London School of Economics Library, Parnell Diary (Coll. Misc. 38).

PRINTED SOURCES

ANSON, Walter Vernon, *The Life of Admiral Lord Anson* (1912).

BARROW, Sir John, *The Life of George, Lord Anson* (1839).

BEARD, G., *Georgian Craftsmen* (1966).

COLVIN, Howard, *A Biographical Dictionary of British Architects 1600–1840* (John Murray, 1978).

G.E.C., *The Complete Peerage*.

CLIFFORD, Sir Thomas & Arthur, *Collectanea Cliffordiana* (Paris, 1817).

CROFT-MURRAY, Edward, *Decorative Painting in England 1537–1837*, II (1970).

GODBER, Joyce, *The Marchioness Grey of Wrest Park*, Bedfordshire Historical Record Society (1968).

GOODISON, Nicholas, 'Mr. Stuart's Tripod', *Burlington Magazine*, October 1972.

HARRIS, Eileen, 'A Flair for the Grandiose – the Architecture of Thomas Wright – II', *Country Life*, 2 September 1971.

HARRIS, Eileen, *Thomas Wright's 'Arbours and Grottoes'* (1979).

HUSSEY, Christopher, 'Shugborough, Staffordshire', *Country Life*, 25 February 1954 *et seq.*

LAING, Alastair, 'O Tempera, O Mores! The Ruin Paintings in the Dining Room at Shugborough', *Apollo*, cxxxvii, April 1993, pp.227–32.

LAING, Alastair, *In Trust for the Nation* (1995), pp.74–5, 201, 236–7.

LEES-MILNE, James, 'Shugborough, Staffordshire', *Connoisseur*, clxv, April and May 1967.

NEALE, J. P., *View of Seats*, 1st Series, III (1820).

NEALE, J. P., *View of Seats*, IV (1821).

PENNANT, Thomas, *Journey from Chester to London* (1782).

PETERS, J. E. C., *Development of Farm Buildings in Western Lowland Staffordshire* (1969).

PITT, William, *A Topographical History of Staffordshire*, II (1817).

ROBINSON, John Martin, *The Wyatts: An Architectural Dynasty* (1979).

ROBINSON, John Martin, *Georgian Model Farms* (1983).

RODGER, Nicholas, *The Admiralty* (1979).

STITT, F. B., 'Admiral Anson at the Admiralty, 1744–62', *Staffordshire Studies*, IV (1991–2), pp.35–76.

STUART, Elizabeth, 'English *Fauteuils à la Reine*: A Set of Seat Furniture by Charles Smith & Company at Shugborough', *National Trust Studies*, 1980, pp.80–93.

WATKIN, David, *Athenian Stuart* (1982).

WILLIAMS, Glyndŵr, Ed., *Documents Relating to Anson's Voyage Round the World* (1967).

WRIGHT, Thomas, *Universal Architecture – Six Original Designs For Arbours* (1755).

FAMILY
TREE

WILLIAM ANSON = Joan, dau. of
of Dunston, Staffs. Barrister | Richard Whitehall or Mitchel
of Lincoln's Inn, bought | of Oldbury, Worcestershire
Shugborough 1624 (d.1644)

WILLIAM ANSON = Elizabeth, dau. of
(c.1628–1688) | Thomas Stafford
| of Bothams Hall, Derbyshire

WILLIAM ANSON = Isabella, dau. and
(1656–1720) | co-heiress of Charles Carrier
| of Wirksworth, Derbyshire

Janette = Sambrooke Adams,   THOMAS ANSON   George Anson = Elizabeth
(1690– | of Sambrooke,   of Shugborough   appointed Rear-Admiral 1745, | Yorke,
1771) | Shropshire   MP for Lichfield   Vice-Admiral 1746, | dau. of Lord
                         (1695–1773)   created *Baron Anson of Soberton* 1747, | (later 1st Earl of)
                         d. unmarried   First Lord of the Admiralty 1747, | Hardwicke
                                      (1697–1762) d.s.p.

GEORGE ADAMS = Mary, dau.
of Orgreave, Staffs. Assumed name and | of 1st Lord Vernon
arms of Anson 1773 (1731–1789) | of Sudbury Hall, Derbyshire
MP for Lichfield

THOMAS ANSON = Anne Margaret, dau. of
MP for Lichfield | Thomas William Coke ('Coke of Norfolk'),
created *Viscount Anson & Baron Soberton* 1806 | afterwards 1st Earl of Leicester, of Holkham,
(1767–1818) | Norfolk

THOMAS WILLIAM ANSON = Louisa Catherine, dau. of
2nd Viscount Anson, created | Nathaniel Philips of Slebech
Earl of Lichfield 1831 (1795–1854) | Hall, Pembrokeshire

THOMAS GEORGE ANSON = Lady Harriet Georgiana Hamilton,
MP for Lichfield | dau. of 1st Duke of Abercorn
2nd Earl of Lichfield (1825–1892)

THOMAS FRANCIS ANSON = Lady Mildred Coke,
3rd Earl of Lichfield | dau. of 2nd Earl of Leicester, of Holkham,
(1856–1918) | Norfolk

THOMAS EDWARD ANSON = (1) Evelyn Maud, dau. of
4th Earl of Lichfield | Col. Edward George Keppel
(1883–1960) | (2) Violet Margaret, dau. of
| Col. Henry Dawson-Greene
| of Whittington Hall, Lancashire

THOMAS WILLIAM ANSON = (1) Anne Ferelith Fenella, dau. of
Viscount Anson | Hon. John Herbert Bowes-Lyon
(1913–1958) | (later married H.R.H. Prince Georg of Denmark)
| (2) Monica, dau. of
| Commander Ralph Neville R.N.

(Thomas) PATRICK JOHN ANSON = Lady Leonora Mary Grosvenor,
5th Earl of Lichfield (b.1939) | dau. of 5th Duke of Westminster

Lady Rose Meriel Margaret   Thomas William Robert   Lady Elouise Anne Elizabeth
(b.1976)   *Viscount Anson*   (b.1981)
                               (b.1978)

INDEX

Page numbers in *italic* refer to illustrations and captions

Abercorn family 49, 69
Abercorn, Louisa, Duchess of 49, 70, 71
Adam, Robert 34
Adams, George, *see* Anson, George Adams
Adams, Thomas 67
Adams & Co., coachmakers 85
Adron, Samuel 37
Alcott, Joseph 37, 40, 55, 71
Alken, Henry 73, 74
Alvanley, Lord 64
Anderson, H. L. 52, 72
Anglesey Abbey 63
Anson, Anne Margaret, Viscountess 34, 42, 64, 67, 68, 69
Anson, Colonel the Hon. Augustus 50, 67
Anson, George, Admiral Lord (1697–1762) *6*, 7–17, 18, 19, 20, 25, 27, 31, 45, 59, 67, 72, 77
Anson, General Sir George (1769–1849) 47, 64
Anson, George Adams (1731–1789) 17, 34, 48
Anson, Lady Elizabeth (*née* Yorke) 15, 16–17, 27, 56, 72
Anson, Lady Louisa May Anne, *see* Tenison
Anson, Mary Adams 71
Anson, Thomas (1695–1773) 17, 18, *18*, 19–20, 21–5, 26, 27–8, 29, 31–3, 45, 46, 48, 49, 75
Anson, Thomas, of Dunston (d.1644) 18
Anson, Thomas II, Viscount (1767–1818) 34–5, 37, 38, 40, 42, 43, 46, 47, 48, 50, 88
Anson, Thomas William, 2nd Viscount, *see* Lichfield, 1st Earl of
Anson, W.V. 72
Anson, William (1656–1720) 7, 18, 68

Anson, General Sir William (1772–1842) 67
Anson family tree 93
Anson Memorial Sword, Sandhurst 50
Antiquities of Athens, The (Stuart) 22, 25, 85
aplustre 25, 90
Arch of Hadrian, Athens 25
Atherstone Hunt 47, 64
Attingham Park 59
Aurora 28, *29*

Bacon, John the Elder 37
Banks, Sir Joseph 82
Barber, Thomas 67, 68
Barker, William 69
Barrow, Sir John 17
Basseggio, Signor 48
Beaudesert 18
Bennett, Frank Moss 67
Bentinck, Lord George 48
Bernard & Co. 60
Bernasconi, Francis 39–40, 71
Blithfield estate 34
Boscawen, Admiral 67
Boulton, Matthew 26, 27, 32, 34, 60, 90
Bowyer, Sir George 72
Brett, Sir Piercy 12, 13, 20–1, 72, 80
Brindley, James 32
Broome Park 38, 39
Brown, Richard 43

Cannock Chase 19, 20, 27
Canton 11, *13*, 20
Cape Finisterre, battle of 7, 13–14, *14*, 31
Carrier, Charles 7
Carrier, Isabella 7
Carshalton 17
Catherine II, Empress of Russia 72
Cavaceppi, Bartolommeo 56
centaurs, Capitoline 33, 56
Centurion, HMS *8*, 9–12, 19, 31, 52, 56, 72, 77
Chalon, A. E. 68

Chamberlin, Mason 71
Chambers, Sir William 74
Choragic Monument of Lysicrates 25–7, 90
Claude 33, 48
Cleveley, John *12*, 77
Coccorante, Leonardo 67
Coke, Anne Margaret, *see* Anson
Coke, Lady Mildred, *see* Lichfield
Coke, Thomas W., 1st Earl of Leicester 34, 42, 43, 46–7, 74
Coke, William 64
Coles, wallpaper 56
Constantine's Column 71
Corsican goats 27, 74, 82
Costa, Angelo Maria 67
Craig, Anne 60
Cunyngham, Daniel 71
Cuyp, Aelbert 33

Dall, Nicholas Thomas *19, 20, 21*, 22, 27, 28, *28*, 29, *29*, 48, 56, 59, 64, 67, 73, 74–5
Dawson-Greene, Margaret, *see* Lichfield
Delaître, Louis 62
Dennis, Captain 31
Derby, William 69
Desan, Karel 67
Desgodetz, Antoine 83
Deval, John the Younger 37, 61
Dick, Sir John 32, 33, 63
Doddington 28, 38
Dupont, Gainsborough *35*

Eastman, Frank 53, 68
Eckhardt & Co., London 38, 61, 64, 69
Eckhardt, Anthony George 78
Eckhardt, Francis Frederick 78
Elis, horse 48, *48*, 73, 74

Fairhaven Collection, Anglesey Abbey 63
Fern Hill, Windsor Great Park 47
Flaxman, John 60
Fowler, John 55, 56, 57, 60, 61

Garrard, George 76
Garrard, Robert 60
George II, King 77
George III, King 72
George IV, King 39–40
Gillert, Richard 90
Gillows of Lancaster 59, 61, 76, 77
Gilpin, William 59
Godde, J. l'aîné 72
Goebel, Karl 69
Gower family, of Trentham 45, 46
Gower, Leveson 45–6
Graham, George 77
Grant, Sir Francis 46, 47, 74
Greenwich Hospital 34, 72
Greville, Thomas 45
Grey, Jemima,
    Marchioness 27, 28, 29, 31, 75, 90
Griffith, Moses 21, 24, 25, 27, 32, 56,
    73, 74–5

Hadrian, Arch of, Athens 25
Hamilton, Lady Harriet Georgiana
    Louisa, see Lichfield
Harding, Chester 67
Harris, Eileen 27, 28, 31
Hawke, Sir Edward 16
Hayter, Sir George 63
Hephaistos, Temple of, Athens 83,
    85
Herring, J. F. 48, 73, 74
Heywood, Charles 79, 80
Hoare, William 59, 77
Holkham 34, 42, 43, 46–7, 74
Honson, Samuel 45
Honthorst, Gerard 32, 63
Hooper, John 90
Horton 29
Howe, Lord 64
Hudson, Thomas 15, 72
Hutchinson, Mrs 8

Jean, Philip 25
Jones, Edward 75
Joubert, Amadée 52
Journey from Chester to London
    (Pennant) 32, 56
Juan Fernandez island 9, 10, 85

Kändler, J. J. 63
Kent, Duchess of 60
Kent, Nathaniel 88
Keppel, Augustus 14, 15
Keppel, Evelyn, see Lichfield
Kirkby, T. 71
Koninck 32

la Jonquière, Marquis de 7, 13–14
Lamerie, Paul de 60
Landseer, Sir Edwin 49, 49, 69, 70
Lane, Samuel 76
Lauri, Filippo 56
Lefroy, Leghorn merchant 33
Le Roy, Julien 63
Leslie, Sir John 69
Lettre sur les découvertes à Hercu-
    laneum (Winckelmann) 29
Lichfield, Evelyn, Countess of 53,
    70
Lichfield, Harriet Georgiana Louisa,
    Countess of 49, 49, 69, 71
Lichfield, Louisa Catherine,
    Countess of 48, 49, 63
Lichfield, Margaret, Countess
    of 53, 54
Lichfield, Mildred, Countess of 51
Lichfield, Patrick John Anson, 5th
    Earl of (b.1939) 52, 54, 54
Lichfield, Thomas Edward Anson,
    4th Earl of (1883–1960) 53, 53–4
Lichfield, Thomas Francis Anson,
    3rd Earl of (1856–1918) 51–2, 51,
    67
Lichfield, Thomas George Anson,
    2nd Earl of (1825–1892) 49–50,
    63, 68
Lichfield, Thomas William Anson,
    1st Earl of (1795–1854) 44, 45–9,
    67
Lichfield, borough of 45–6
Lichfield House, St James's
    Square, 17, 47, 49
Lichfield Race Course 48
Livermere Park 37
Lock, Matthias 56, 59
Lord Anson's Hunt 47, 47, 63–4
Loutherbourg, Philip de 67
Lyme Park 52

Mackell, John 41
McMeeken, farm steward 50
Massé, Jules 69
Mead, Dr Richard 33, 48
Melbourne, Lord 45, 47
Meléndez, Miguel Jacinto 63
Mlinaric, David 68, 77
Moisy of Paris, clock movement 63
Montigny, Philippe-Claude 57
Moor Park, Middlesex 17
Morant & Boyd, decorators 50, 61,
    71
Moser, G. M. 77
Motte, Sir Lister 45

Munby, Alan 54

Nesfield, W. A. 79
Neville, John 60
Nollekens, Joseph 32, 33, 33, 56,
    62, 76
Norbury, Mr 64
Nuestra Señora de Covadonga 12,
    12, 77
Nuthall Temple 28

Oakedge 56
Osterley Park 59

Padbery, Andrew 64
Paget, William 18
Palazzo Barberini, Rome 33
Paltronieri, Pietro 59
Parita, Santa Fé 10–11, 11
Parnell, Sir John 18
Pennant, Thomas 20, 32, 73, 83, 85
Phillips, Thomas 44, 57
Piranesi, Giambattista 29, 31
Pitt, William 43, 88
Pond, Arthur 67
Poussin, Nicolas 31, 83
Prince George, HMS 64

Quiberon Bay, battle of 16, 64

Ramsay, Allan 67
Ranton Abbey estate 46, 47, 49,
    52, 74
Rebecca, Biagio 38, 59
Reinagle, R. R. 74
Rembrandt van Rijn 32, 48
Reni, Guido 28, 29, 32, 57, 63
Revett, Nicholas 25, 85
Reynolds, Sir Joshua 6, 14, 71, 72
Richmond, Duke of 72
Riesener, J. H. 62
Roggen, clock movements 59
Romer, Emick 60
Rosa da Tivoli 67
Rose, Joseph the
    Younger 37, 55, 61, 68
Rosebery, Anna Margaret,
    Countess 64, 67
Rossi, Charles 37, 39, 41, 71
Royal Buck Hounds, Windsor 47,
    64
Rubestuck, François 63
Runciman, Steven 50

St James's Square, London 17,
    47, 49

Salomé, Anthony de 71
Sandhurst 50
Sandon estate 34
Saunders, Admiral Sir Charles 72
Scarpellino's, Rome 62
Scheemakers, Peter 25, 57, 83, 85, 90
Schmidt, Joseph 62
Scott, Samuel *14*
Sefton, Lord 47
Seward, Anna 21
Seward, Dr 32
Sharp, Robert 60
Shugborough: *Exterior*: East
    front *4, 32, 36,* 56, 75; Façade 34–
    5, 39; Portico 25, 26; slate
    cladding 36–7, 53–4; South
    Wing 38; West front 29, 38, 39,
    54, 75; *Interior*: Anson Room 77;
    Ante Room 56–7, *57*; Bird
    Room 37, 68–9, *68*; Blue
    Drawing Room 50, 52, *60*, 61;
    Boudoir 78; Bust Parlour 56;
    Dining Room 28–9, *28*, 38, 57–
    60, *58*; Entrance Hall 37, 55–6, *55*;
    Library 29, *30*, 75–6, *76*; Red
    Drawing Room 37, 37–8, 61–4,
    62; Saloon 38–40, *39*, 71–2;
    Staircase Hall and Landing 64–8,
    65, 66; State Bedroom 50,
    69, *70*, 71; State Sitting
    Room 69–70; Swallow Passage
    52, 64; Verandah Room and
    Passage 47, 72–5; *Gardens* 20–
    2, 79–85, *80, 84*; Kitchen
    Garden 43, 88; Rose Garden 83–
    5, *84*; Wild Garden 79; *Park and
    Monuments* 19, 27, 40–2, 64, 74,
    85–90; Blue Bridge 79; Cat's
    Monument 82, *82*, 83; Chinese
    House 20–1, *21*, 48, 52, 61, 79–80;
    Dairy 42–3, 86; Doric Temple
    83, 85; Druid 79; Essex Bridge
    19, *32*, 83; Estate 40, 54; Lanthorn
    of Demosthenes 26–7, *26*, 74, *89*,
    90; Lichfield Lodge 40, 41, *41*;
    model cottages 41–2, *41*; North
    Walk 79; Orangery 22, 83, 85;
    Pagoda 21, 41, 74; Park Farm 19,
    40, 42–3, 50, 88; Ruins 20, *20*, 56,
    79, *81*; Shepherd's Monument 31,
    31, 83; Stables 85; Stafford
    Lodge 41; Tower of the Winds
    24, 25, 42, 43, 52, 54, 61, 64, 69, 75,
    85–8, *86, 87*; Triumphal Arch
    22, 23, 25, 90, *90*; White Barn
    Farm 42, *42*, 88; Yew Tree 83

Sieber, Ernest 60
Six Original Designs for Arbours
    (Wright) 31
Smith, Charles & Co. 50, 61, 69,
    71, 76
Smith, Daniel 60
Social Welfare Association 52
Society of Dilettanti 25, 31, 49
Society for the Reformation of
    Juvenile Offenders 49
Solom, Anton 71
South Carolina 7–8
Staffordshire County Council 54
Staffordshire County Museum 54,
    85
Staffordshire Longhorns 50, *50*
Storr, Paul 60
Stuart, James 'Athenian' 19, 22, *22*,
    24, 25, *25*, 26, 26–7, *27*, 31, *32*, 34,
    36, 52, 61, 62, 63, 64, 67, 83, 85, 86,
    90
Summer Palace, Peking 61
Sussex, Duke of 47
sweet pea, Anson 10, *10*, 85

Tatton Park 28, 38
Tenison, Lady Louisa Mary
    Anne 50–1
Thesion, Athens 83, 85
Thomas, Graham Stuart 83
threshing machines, water-
    powered 42
Tixall estate 34, 64
Trinity House, London 37
tripods, significance of 26
Trubshaw, Charles Cope 85

Underwood & Co. 64
Uxbridge, Earl of 47

Van de Velde 33
Vanderbank, John *18*, 57, 64, *66*, 72
Vangelder, Peter Mathias 37
Vassalli, stuccoist 28, 29, *29*,
    57, 72, 75
Venables, George 45
Vernon, Mary 71
Victoria, Princess 47
Vitali, Candido 67

Walpole, Horace 16
Ward, Charlotte Blakeney 69
Ward, James 73
Warreley, James and Thomas 85
Watt, James 34
Waymouth, Nigel *54*

Weaver, Thomas 73, 74
Webb, William 47, 63, 73, 74
Wedgwood, Josiah 26–7, 32, 34, 90
Westmacott, Richard the
    Younger 37, 61
Wheelock, Mr 43
Whitby, Thomas 18
William IV, King 72
William Salt Library, Stafford 48
Wilton, Joseph 56
Wimpole Hall 16
Winterton, Georgiana, Countess of
    71
Wright, Thomas 27, 28–9, *29*, 31,
    38, 57, 64, 75, 79, 82, 83
Wyatt, Benjamin 36
Wyatt family 51–2
Wyatt, Harvey 51, 77
Wyatt, James 34, 38, 39
Wyatt, Robert Harvey I 51
Wyatt, Robert Harvey II 51, 52
Wyatt, Samuel 34–40, *35, 36, 38,*
    41, *41,* 42, 43, 53, 55, 56, 59, 61, 62,
    64, 65, 68, 69, 71, 86, 88
Wyatt, William 51
'Wyatt Window' 56

Yorke, Lady Elizabeth *see* Anson,
    Lady Elizabeth
Yorke, Philip, 1st Earl of
    Hardwicke 16, 28, 59

Zuccarelli, Francesco 50, 61